The Olympics at 100:

A Celebration in Pictures

U.S. figure skater Nancy Kerrigan beams after completing her free skating program at the 1994 Winter Games. She won the silver medal.

Vitaly Scherbo of the Unified Team performs on the rings at Barcelona. He won his fourth gymnastics gold medal.

The Olympics at 100:

A Celebration in Pictures

Larry Siddons
The Associated Press

ABOVE LEFT: The USA's Gail Devers crossed the finish line for a gold medal, a split second ahead of Juliet Cuthbert of Jamaica, in the 100 meters in Barcelona.

LEFT: American speedskater Dan Jansen takes a victory lap with his daughter, Jane, after winning the gold medal in world record time in the 1,000 meters in the 1994 Winter Games in Norway.

ABOVE RIGHT: U.S. swimmer Mark Spitz wins the 200-meter butterfly final at the 1972 Olympics in Munich.

MACMILLAN
USA

AP Project Director: Norm Goldstein
Editor: Barbara Gilson
Photo Researchers: Maura Lynch, Jim Supanick
© The Associated Press, 1995
ISBN 0-02-860346-X

To Andrew
To Gordo, who taught me sports writing was fun.

ACKNOWLEDGMENTS

If everyone who had a hand in researching and writing this book were listed, it probably would stand as a volume by itself. All were invaluable, but I would like to express special thanks to Peter Diamond, Laura Olsen, Bob Brennan, Dick Yarbrough, Jennifer Jordan, Michele Verdier, Mike Moran, Fekrou Kidane, Andrew Napier, Steve Wilson, Morley Myers, Steve Parry, John Rodda, David Miller, Dick Pound, Kevan Gosper, Lee Jae-hong, Caroline Serle, Jose Sotello, Jeff Tishman, Mark Mandel, Anita DeFrantz, Harvey Schiller, John Krimsky, LeRoy Walker, Vitaly Smirnow, Billy Payne, Charlie Battle, Doug Gatlin, Ann Duncan, Bob Condron, Gayle Bodin, Jeff Cravens, Mike Janofsky, John Feinstein, Luan Peszek, Charlie Snyder, Pete Cava and Guido Tognoni; J.M. Ker, for constant advice and direction; my colleagues and friends at the AP, most notably Darrell Christian, Terry Taylor, Ron Sirak and Rick Warner; my editors, Norm Goldstein at the AP and Barbara Gilson at Arco, who never ranted but always made it better; and my family, who put up with too many days when I was off tracing the Five Rings.

BELOW: American figure skater Tonya Harding cries as she shows the judges the problem with her laces during her free skate program at the 1994 Winter Games. She was allowed to restart her program.

ABOVE: Thomas Johansson (in blue), of Sweden, loses to American Jeff Blatnick in super-heavyweight Greco-Roman wrestling. Johansson won the silver, but had to forfeit the medal after testing positive for steroids.

Right: China's Fu Mingxia during the women's 10-meter platform diving competition in Barcelona. The 13-year-old won the gold.

Above: Carl Lewis leaps to a gold medal in the long jump at the 1988 Games in Seoul.

Far Right: Atlantans celebrate the announcement of their city as host of the 1996 Games.

Contents

Carl Lewis takes the baton from U.S. teammate Calvin Smith in the 400 relay at the 1984 Games.

ABOVE: Billy Payne, president of the Atlanta Committee Olympic Games, signs one of the 200,000 applications for volunteers for the 1996 Games. At left is Linda Stephenson, managing director for Olympic programs, and, at right, Ginger Watkins, managing director of corporate services for ACOG.

BELOW: Atlanta officials prepare to present their city as Olympic host before the International Olympic Committee meeting in Tokyo in 1990. From the left: Mayor Maynard Jackson, delegation head Billy Payne, and former Mayor Andrew Young.

CHAPTER I

Going for the Gold

The breakfast room at the Palace Hotel in Lausanne, Switzerland, is less a room than a stage, and on a

golden morning in late summer of 1990 Billy Payne was working that stage like an old trouper.

It was the final month of a race Payne had been running for more than three years, a contest with five other cities to host the biggest event in the world: The 100th birthday of the Olympic Games.

It would be a celebration of athletic excellence and mass marketing virtually guaranteed to generate billions of dollars and leave the winner with a sports and economic legacy for generations to come. When Payne and Atlanta had joined the chase, the conventional wisdom was, "Good luck, but forget it." Athens, the site of the first modern Games in 1896 and the capital of the land that gave birth to the Olympics 2,000 years before, was a lock. Tradition would carry the day.

It wasn't just the Acropolis and ancient Olympia that William Porter Payne, a former All-American end at the University of Georgia, and his fellow Bulldogs had to counter. The votes to award the centennial Games were in the hands of the 87 members of the International Olympic Committee, a group of business leaders, government officials, ex-athletes and crowned heads who took their traditions very seriously.

They enjoyed their comforts and perks, too. The chance to sun on a Mediterranean beach or have dinner with royalty often meant more in their decisions than new stadiums or arenas, and Atlanta—the glass-and-chrome capital of the New South—had a definite lack of sandy cabanas or ancestral homes.

"That's one of our problems," Payne said. "These other cities have kings and queens. We've got Prince and the Duke of Earl."

No rock 'n' roll icons were breakfasting at the Palace that sun-splashed day, but just about everyone else got a visit from Payne along with the strong French coffee and flaky croissants. Blue blazer and red tie flying, Payne jumped from table to table, presenting one more piece of the pitch for Atlanta's bid to the IOC members who had gathered for meetings at the committee's marble-lined headquarters on the shores of Lake Geneva.

Payne was at ease, dealing with people he had come to know well as he and his team of Georgia lawyers, doctors and wheeler-dealers hopscotched the globe in search of support. What a change from the nervousness of the early days, when anyone standing outside a conference room or even in the lobby of a hotel where the IOC was meeting could expect to be approached by a tall, bespectacled man with dark hair, have a large hand thrust toward them and hear, "Hi! I'm Billy Payne," in a deep Southern drawl, even if that greeting had been offered just five minutes earlier.

That was then, in a snowstorm in Vienna or a foggy day at Frankfurt airport. This was now, on a balmy Swiss summer morning, and next month would come The Vote. On September 18, in a Tokyo hotel, the IOC would cast secret ballots to decide among Athens, Atlanta, Belgrade, Manchester, Melbourne and Toronto as the host of its big birthday bash.

Just as the setting had changed, the sure thing had turned into a horse race. Somewhere along the way, tradition had collided with real life, and conventional wisdom tangled with dollars and cents. And you could sense that Payne felt his side was right where it wanted to be—not just closing fast, but in front with the finish line in sight.

"People said we were out of our minds," recalled Payne. "But we sincerely believed that we could provide the proper setting for this great celebration. We believed that we could create something here that would not only serve the Olympic Games but give something back to the community. And we really did, from the first day, believe we could win."

Payne's Olympic odyssey began after he helped raise money for a building at St. Luke's church in suburban Dunwoody, Georgia. The campaign was so successful, he felt, that the people of the community—and the bigger community of Atlanta—should dedicate themselves to something bigger that could unite a diverse region. And it needed some unification just then.

Atlanta was a success story that had fallen on hard times. It first sprang up as a railroad town in the early 1800s and was prospering when the Civil War began. It swelled during the war as a main supply center for the Confederacy, and thus became a target for Union troops as they pushed southward. In 1864, armies led by General William Tecumseh Sherman marched through Atlanta and burned it to the ground.

A century later, it rose like a phoenix from the ashes of the Old South of Jefferson and Lee. It became the center of the New South, a civil rights hotbed that also attracted big corporations and boasted one of the biggest in the world as an anchor of local commerce—the Coca-Cola Co., with its massive workforce and annual budget in the billions.

By the 1970s, if you looked in the dictionary under success, you'd probably see a map of Atlanta.

But the good times didn't last forever. The glitz faded. Crime rose. The downtown of glittering steel and glass towers, and the subterranean shops and restaurants of Underground Atlanta, didn't look quite so appealing. The city that billed itself as "too busy to hate" in its upswing became increasingly segregated, a black core of dilapidated public housing and second-rate shopping surrounded by pristine white suburbs, with big lawns and shopping malls spreading farther and farther away from Peachtree Street.

Many would look at the scene and say it was hopeless. Payne and his friends saw reason for lots of hope. What they needed was a hook, something to get people interested in rebuilding Atlanta once again. Something big, something special, something they had never done before.

Like hosting the Olympics. And why not go for the big one—the Games of 1996, the 100th anniversary of their modern birth?

Of course, most people figured that those Games were going one place and one place only—back to Athens, the site of the first of the modern festivals. The Greek capital made no secret of its desire to have the Games, and, indeed, said on more than one occasion that it had a sort of priority to serve as the host.

But no one said the Games *had* to be in Athens, and there were good reasons not to stage them there. The city was dirty and crowded. Streets were crumbling and athletic facilities for the most part were second-rate. Perhaps most important, the Greek economy was shaky and the government tended to veer from left-wing socialism to reactionary dictatorship and back.

Around the world, cities started to look at the race for '96 as wide open, and joined in the chase. And in 1987, Payne and his friends jumped in, too, forming a group to go after the big show.

The core group of Payne, Ginger Watkins and Linda Stephenson, three long-time acquaintances, began lining up support. One of their first converts was Cindy Fowler, a leading community volunteer. The group soon was being called "Billy and the Girl Scouts."

They won over two of Atlanta's biggest names, Maynard Jackson and Andrew Young, who both served as mayors. Both had been active in the civil rights movement of Dr. Martin Luther King Jr., and Young had been U.S. Ambassador to the United Nations. Those connections were to prove invaluable in Atlanta's efforts.

The IOC picks host cities, but not every city that wants to serve as host gets to make its case to the IOC. It first must be picked as the representative of its national Olympic committee. Payne and his group took their bid to the U.S. Olympic Committee, and in April 1988, just before the Seoul Olympics, the USOC chose Atlanta to carry the U.S. bid for 1996.

In the next few months, Payne and his group traveled the world. They were late entries in the race for the centennial Games, and they knew they had a lot of ground to make up—and misgivings to overcome.

One was Athens, although that city's grip on the No. 1 spot was slipping as more and more negatives came up.

Another was 1984. The United States had hosted the Games just four years previously, and the IOC liked to move the Olympics around. The Los Angeles Games were successful, leaving that big $230 million surplus. But they also left a bad taste in the mouth of some IOC members, who felt the Los Angeles organizers—and particularly committee chief Peter V. Ueberroth—had concentrated too much on the bottom line at some cost to the Olympic spirit.

And a third obstacle was crime. Atlanta had become, in that hearty perennial of tabloid headlines, the "murder capital of the world." The specter of rampant street crime had to be dispelled.

Payne figured the best way to fight these negatives was to get out and meet the people who would be doing the voting, and bring as many of them as possible to Atlanta to see for themselves what he and his friends were so proud of.

Wherever there was a meeting of the IOC or some related group, you could count on Payne or one of his associates, such as Watkins or Charlie Battle, being there. Most of the bidding cities did the same thing, but Atlanta had an ace up its sleeve in Andy Young, and he became actively involved. The former UN ambassador started to look up old friends, especially in Africa and the Middle East. They, in turn, helped Young reach vital IOC members and enabled him to make his pitch. This was crucial.

By late 1988, two years before the IOC vote, there was a crowded field of eight finalists. It was unlikely that any city, therefore, would get the required majority of the 86 IOC members on the first ballot, so bidders had to build a solid base they knew would stick with them through the balloting, and back that up with voters who might favor another city but were willing to switch if that bidder was eliminated.

A city never was picked to host an Olympics based on sports alone.

There's so much more involved—public support, good highways, a telephone system that works, an airport that can handle the hundreds of thousands of visitors that an Olympics lures.

Your city can have the best stadiums, the fastest running tracks, superb gymnasiums. But if it does not also have splendid hotels, fine restaurants, and fancy shops, then forget it.

Remember: Athletes don't vote on the Olympic host. Members of the IOC do, and those members like the finer things of life. Most also have husbands or wives who need to be entertained while the Games are going on, and a suite in a four-star hotel or a trip to a designer boutique can sure help pass the time.

This is a lesson all bidding cities learn quickly if they hope to be successful. As with any election, it pays to know who your voters are and what they like.

The basics are these:

A city must show the willingness to turn itself over to the IOC for 16 days. It must have enough money—about $1.5 billion for the Summer Games, a half-billion less for the Winter—to pay for first-class venues and events. It should have some sporting tradition, and a link to the Olympic movement always helps. Perhaps more than anything, it should have the support of its people, to avoid the kind of public hassles and headaches that can embarrass the IOC. The committee doesn't want another situation like 1976, when Denver pulled out as host of the Winter Games at the last minute after citizens passed a referendum saying they didn't want the responsibility.

The bidding process has become more formalized in recent years. The IOC sends an evaluation team to each bidding city and receives a report grading the hopefuls in areas ranging from size of the main stadiums to quality of hotels and how long it takes to get to the airport from downtown.

Each city must also submit a bid book. These are elaborate things, containing vital statistics but also a lot of glossy pictures and propaganda. They cost hundreds of thousands of dollars to print and distribute. Each IOC member gets a copy, and for the most part they go unread. "There are four categories of deception," USOC president LeRoy Walker liked to say. "Lies, damn lies, statistics and bid books."

For years, the IOC had little problem picking the hosts for the Games because so few cities bid. They were scared by high costs (Montreal) or being targets for international politics (Munich) or just saw the Olympics as a hassle to avoid.

That changed with Los Angeles in 1984 and the $230 million profit it turned. The money went to fund continuing American sports programs but the attention the Games focused on Los Angeles and the bright picture of Southern California that they presented to the world caught the attention of other cities around the globe.

Suddenly, bidding for the Games became a hot ticket. There were 14 cities—seven summer, seven winter—lined up when the IOC voted in 1986 to place the '92 Games in Albertville, France, and Barcelona, Spain. That bidding became hot and heavy—and very expensive, particularly in the race for the Summer Olympic site.

Barcelona was considered a shoo-in because it was home to the IOC's president, Juan Antonio Samaranch. Paris, however, thought it deserved the honor of hosting the Games in the centenary year of Baron de Coubertin's first call for the Games to be revived. Both cities, and many of their rivals, went wild, showering IOC members with lavish gifts.

There were hotel suites and first-class air tickets whenever a member wanted to drop by. Lots of food and lots of wine. And maybe a little something left in your room when you returned from a gruelling round of lunch, dinner and cocktails. Like the fur coats some members received from Paris. Or the jewelry that Barcelona gave away, worth thousands of dollars apiece.

"I even happen to know the shoe size of the second daughter of a certain IOC member," said Sir Robert Scott, who headed Manchester's unsuccessful bids for 1996 and 2000.

Some of the freebies were one of a kind—like a heart operation, provided at a leading French hospital for an IOC member from a Third World nation. When Cuba's IOC member, Gonzalez Guerra, visited Atlanta, he mentioned that the bulldog, mascot of Payne's alma mater of Georgia, was his favorite canine but unavailable in his homeland. Guerra didn't have to bark twice. Payne made sure there was a bulldog heading back to Cuba when Guerra returned to Havana.

All told, the '92 bidders officially spent about $100 million and who knows how much unofficially. Paris spent at least $40 million, including a lavish buffet for several hundred people at an IOC meeting in Seoul; Barcelona was close behind in its spending, and barely pulled off the victory.

The IOC was embarrassed by the extravagance—how else would you describe a party in Germany at which the bidding committee from Brisbane offered Australian lamb, flown all the way from Queensland courtesy of media magnate Rupert Murdoch?—and placed restrictions on public spending by bidders.

The parties stopped, but the gifts did not. They just became more subtle.

Other Bidders

To win the right to host the 1996 Olympics, Atlanta had to run a gauntlet of rivals—and then run it again.

The two-tiered process started with the U.S. Olympic Committee, which would pick the American representative in the bidding. A dozen cities submitted proposals, with Minneapolis-St. Paul, at the head of the list when the bidding started in 1986.

Minnesota's Twin Cities were on a roll. They had just hosted baseball's World Series, where the hometown Twins won the championship in the spanking new Metrodome downtown. Other new arenas were being built or in the planning stages. The region's economy, led by the Pillsbury baking company, was booming. And the citizens were sports crazy.

Other cities hoping for the USOC's nod included San Francisco and Nashville, Tennessee.

But Atlanta's late-starting bid caught up with the Twin Cities and all the others, and won overwhelmingly in a vote by the USOC's executive board in Washington, D.C., on April 29, 1988.

From there, it was on to the Big One— the International Olympic Committee.

By the deadline in late 1988, Atlanta was among six cities from around the world that had registered with the IOC as bidders for '96. The others, with a quick look at their strengths and weaknesses, were:

ATHENS, GREECE

Plus—The traditional favorite, site of the 1896 Games and the capital of the country were the ancient Olympics took place.

Minus—A crowded, polluted city. Poor public transportation. Shaky economy and a history of unstable government.

BELGRADE, YUGOSLAVIA

Plus—A love of sports, with a history of staging world championships and the memory of the very successful Winter Games in Sarajevo in 1984.

Minus—Political instability and economic collapse. Facilities in desperate need of repair or replacement.

MANCHESTER, ENGLAND

Plus—Prosperous economy and stable government, although reluctant to support the bid. A long history of Olympic tradition and championships. Close to London and all its attractions.

Minus—Few stadiums or arenas built. Questions about funding the construction and operations. And, as many tourists could tell you, rainy summer weather.

MELBOURNE, AUSTRALIA

Plus—Good range of existing facilities and solid plans for construction of new ones. A central Olympic Village for all athletes. Government support and a sports-mad population.

Minus—It's a long, long flight from just about anywhere in the rest of the world.

Melbourne also had hosted an Olympics before, in 1956, the only Games held in the Southern Hemisphere.

TORONTO, CANADA

Plus—State-of-the-art facilities, topped by the SkyDome, the baseball-football stadium with the retractable roof. A polyglot population that made Toronto one of the world's most cosmopolitan cities.

Minus—Weak economy. Memories of Montreal's billion-dollar debt in 1976. Vocal public opposition from groups who said Toronto should concentrate on housing and jobs for the poor, not sports for the rich.

ABOVE: Atlanta Mayor Maynard Jackson receives congratulations from IOC President Juan Antonio Samaranch after the Georgia city won the bid to host the 1996 Games.

BELOW: Juan Antonio Samaranch speaks at a reception celebrating Atlanta's successful bid to host the Games. From left: Billy Payne, Gov. Joe Frank Harris and former Mayor Andrew Young.

CHAPTER II

The Winner is ...

The IOC gathered in Tokyo in 1990 to select the site for its birthday bash.

Out in the Pacific, a typhoon was building. It would hit the capital about 24 hours after the vote on the

LEFT: Maynard Jackson, then Atlanta mayor, gives the thumbs-up sign after the city won the bid.

1996 host city, scheduled to be announced at 8 p.m. September 18, dousing the streets and blowing the trees but having little long-term effect.

In that way, the IOC decision would create a much bigger whirlpool.

It was hard to tell just how the vote would go. IOC members usually love to talk and exchange thoughts and ideas. But as the balloting got closer, they were strangely quiet.

"I honestly think most of the members remain undecided," Augustin Arroyo, a veteran IOC member from Ecuador, said a few nights before the vote. "What makes them decide? It's different for everyone. It depends what details they pay attention to, what are their interests."

Oddsmakers agreed on one thing—Belgrade had no chance whatsoever. They said the same thing two years earlier about the chances of Lillehammer, Norway, to host the 1994 Winter Games. Lillehammer won that vote.

Everybody seemed to have a last-minute trick, and the Greeks angered their rivals by playing fast and loose with the rules. First, they rented a suite of offices in the IOC hotel, which was supposed to be off-limits to bidders. Then, the Greek government held a big party, featuring singer Nina Mousskoni. Technically, this was OK, since the Athens bid was not the official host. But when was the last time someone from the Greek Embassy invited you to have retsina and souvlaki on a September night in Tokyo?

On the morning of the vote, each bidding city made a final, formal presentation to the IOC. In a blind draw, Atlanta went first.

The presentation included speeches by Payne, Andrew Young, Mayor Maynard Jackson and Georgia Governor Joe Bob Harris. It also featured a videotaped message from President George Bush. Jackson said he was pleased with the way his city had performed, no matter how the vote turned out. "We feel we can produce the kind of Olympics for the next 100 years," he said, "and make the world proud."

Most of the presentations followed similar lines. Melbourne's included a satellite link to a big party being staged at the National Tennis Center, site of the Australian Open, and featured a live duet of a jazz clarinetist and an aboriginal digerido. Manchester had a speech from Britain's Princess Anne, a former Olympic equestrian competitor and an IOC member.

Athens struck a nerve. IOC members had been complaining for several weeks of a growing arrogance from the Greek capital. The presentation went smoothly, although members asked in great detail about Athens' air pollution, traffic jams and security. But at the news conference afterward, things got testy, with Greek Prime Minister Constantine Mitsotakis and Lambis Nikalou, an IOC member, criticizing reporters' questions. "We did not spend our time saying, 'Athens should have the Games,'" said the city's bid chairman, Spyros Metaxa. "We made practical arguments. Tonight, if we win, I will be very proud."

Pride often does go before a fall, and that night Athens hit with a thud. At 8:47 p.m. Tokyo time, IOC president Juan Antonio Samaranch stepped before the microphones

ABOVE: Construction starts on the Olympic Village site near the Georgia Tech campus.

and cameras in a vast conference hall and ripped open a sealed envelope containing the outcome of the vote.

IOC rules call for a victor to get a simple majority of all votes cast. If a winner is not determined on the first ballot, the low vote-getter drops out, and another round is taken. It goes on—with a different color of ballot for each round—until one city goes over the top. On this night in Tokyo, there were 86 voting members—Samaranch does not cast a ballot unless there's a tie—so a city needed at least 44 votes to win.

The race was so close, with so many qualified cities, that it took the members the maximum five ballots to decide. A touch of the nose by Flor Isava-Fonseca, an IOC member from Venezuela, signaled Atlanta that it had made it to the final two, but it had no idea of the outcome.

"And the winner is," Samaranch said. The big room was silent.

Samaranch paused. Then came the word. "Atlanta!"

ABOVE: The superstructure for the stands at the Olympic Stadium starts to take shape in 1994.

In Tokyo, Maynard Jackson held his hands in prayer. Back home, 14 hours behind, fireworks filled the morning sky over Peachtree Street and Atlanta rocked with the cheers of new Olympic hosts.

Belgrade had been knocked out on the first ballot. Next went Manchester. Athens led on rounds 1 and 2, but Atlanta caught up on round 3, when Melbourne was eliminated, and that was the key.

"Once Melbourne left, there was only Athens and two North American cities, Atlanta and Toronto," said IOC member Kevan Gosper of Australia. "At that point, the members had to decide if they wanted Europe or North America. Those who wanted North America decided they wanted Atlanta."

On the fourth round, Atlanta surged in front, but was still shy of a majority. It won on the final round, picking up most of the 22 votes that Toronto previously held.

"IT'S ATLANTA!!!" the big banner headline on that day's Atlanta *Journal and Constitution* proclaimed.

"I feel like an exclamation point has been laid down in the history of our city and the history of the world," Jackson said. "This is not about money and all the stadiums we can build. It's about the values for which Olympism stands, and it shows we have learned our lessons about equality and fair play."

Immediately, beaten rivals cried foul. Often, their criticism contained a reference to a popular soft drink. "These will be the Coca-Cola Olympics," said Melina Mercouri, the Oscar-winning actress who had become a Greek government minister and a key figure in the Athens bid.

Others said much the same thing. Schoolchildren in Australia voted to boycott Coke, and in Athens cans of the soft drink were cracked open and poured into sewers.

It was a complaint that Atlanta had heard before. Coke has been one of the Olympics' biggest corporate sponsors since the early part of the century, and the argument went that having the 1996 Games in its hometown would be good for the company—and, in turn, good for the IOC. Almost before the cheers had died, Payne and his cohorts were on the defensive about the Coke connection.

The next day, in a session with a handful of reporters, Payne went to great lengths to say that, yes, Atlanta and Coke were related but, no, Coke did not buy the Olympics for its hometown.

"We have never received a single penny from the Coca-Cola Co.," Payne repeated over and over. (Like any good Atlantan, he pronounced it, "Co-Cola.") He also mentioned repeatedly that local Coca-Cola bottling companies and distributors had contributed to just about every one of the rival bids.

So, if it wasn't Coke's money, how DID Atlanta get the Games?

Dollars did have something to do with it, if not from soft drinks than from television and sponsorships. TV rights provide a sizeable chunk of the IOC budget and the biggest portion of that comes from U.S. networks. Games in the United States, especially in the Eastern time zone, provide more live prime-time programming and a good chance for higher ratings, and therefore offer networks the chance to charge more for commercial time. More money from commercials means higher rights fees. For Atlanta, NBC wound up with the U.S. television rights in exchange for a record $456 million—$55 million more than it paid for the 1992 Games in Barcelona. (CBS got U.S. broadcast rights to the 1998 Winter Games in Nagano, Japan, for $375 million.)

Marketing sponsors also find a U.S.-based Olympics more attractive, since it gives them a more direct link to their biggest, most lucrative markets. Sponsorship, especially through its $40-million-a-shot plan of worldwide marketing rights in select categories such as telecommunications and photography, is a growing source of IOC income.

But the secret to Atlanta's successful bid went way beyond money. Its bid, after all, only cost $7.1 million, compared with $30 million for Athens. Everything Atlanta had to offer was first class, from stadiums to hotels to airports. The IOC evaluation commission graded it at or near the top of every one of its review categories. The facilities it already had—such as the Omni for volleyball, the Georgia Dome for basketball and gymnastics and the mammoth World Congress Center for a multitude of minor sports—were unsurpassed, and plans for facilities that had to be built were top quality without being ostentatious.

"We had to decide if we were going to move forward or we were going to look back," said Richard Pound, a Montreal lawyer and one of the IOC's most influential members. "Athens had the tradition. But were we then going to say, 'This is where we were in 1896, and this is how we dressed in 1896,' and so on. In the end, we looked forward."

Atlanta was able to build an unshakable support base. These votes used to be decided just like the United Nations, on an East-West split. But by the time of the Tokyo vote, the Berlin Wall was tumbling and old blocs no longer existed. That meant Belgrade lacked a natural constituency. Athens never expanded on its foundation of traditionalists. The votes of the British Commonwealth were split three ways, among Manchester, Melbourne and Toronto. That left the rest of the world for Atlanta, and Young did a marvelous job of lining up the growing segment of IOC members from Africa, the Middle East and other scattered areas.

"I've been in 15 foreign cities with Andy," Payne once said, "and I haven't yet been in one where he wasn't recognized on the street."

And Payne made sure that the IOC got what it loves the most—personal attention, down to the finest point. "Detail is what matters in this effort," he said, "and we are very, very good at that."

Of the 86 members who voted in Tokyo, 70 had visited Atlanta and gotten a taste of Southern hospitality, 1990s style.

"People were surprised by Atlanta and what a great place it is," said Bob Brennan, ACOG's press chief. "Most people don't know much about the South except what they see in *Gone With the Wind*. They found Atlanta is a modern, progressive city with very friendly people."

Is Everybody Happy?

The Olympics can be a carrot. Organizers can plead their case to a reluctant citizenry by saying that without the Olympics, they won't get that new expressway/commuter train/airport/business investment. Conversely, disparate groups can latch onto the Olympics to try to get their ends met. When Melbourne was bidding for the '96 Games, the cause was forwarded as an antidote for everything that might upset the city. It got so bad that an editorial cartoon showed a reluctant child frowning at his dinner plate, and his mother screaming: "If you don't eat your cabbage, Melbourne won't get the Olympics!"

But the Games can be a whipping boy as well, and Atlanta's vocal critics quickly took aim.

Construction of venues was one of the prime targets. Most of the Olympic building, especially the big new venues like the swimming hall, the Olympic village and the main stadium, were headed for some of the poorest parts of the city—the notorious Techwood public housing projects near Georgia Tech and the area south of Atlanta-Fulton County Stadium, between the downtown and Hartsfield International Airport. Community activists jumped on Payne, accusing him of ignoring their constituencies. Payne, with the help of Jackson and Young, brought those communities into the decision-making process and, with some modifications, received final clearance for the stadiums and halls. In return, ACOG pledged to increase minority hiring; a report issued at the end of 1992 showed that 33.2 percent of the committee's employees were black, with 58 percent of the total jobs held by women. That's a significant number in an organization that will eventually employ some 63,000 people—more than any other business in Georgia, even Coke.

Environmentalists had an equally sharp impact. They argued that plans to develop a multi-sports Olympic park at Stone Mountain, east of the city, would upset the ecology of a wildlife setting within easy reach of millions of Atlantans. They were especially upset by a plan to literally suck up an island in the middle of one of the park's lakes, build the rowing course there, then replace the island once the Games were finished. That plan was dropped and the rowing course moved to Lake Lanier. Also scrapped were plans for an equestrian center at Stone Mountain; those events were shifted to an existing equestrian facility.

Perhaps the loudest protests—or at least the ones that reached all the way to Lausanne—came from gay rights activists. Volleyball preliminary rounds originally were scheduled for Marietta, Georgia, a conservative, overwhelmingly white suburb and the home of House Speaker Newt Gingrich. In 1993, Marietta voters passed a resolution condemning gay lifestyles. Homosexual and lesbian groups were outraged and threatened to lead a boycott of the Games if the volleyball venue remained there. ACOG stood firm, until Samaranch and other IOC members hinted that the protests should be listened to. The volleyball preliminaries were moved out of Marietta.

As the preparation for the Games moved into its final year, not all the critics had been silenced.

"I think we've lost a once-in-a-lifetime opportunity," said the Rev. Timothy McDonald, who heads the Atlanta Olympic Conscience Coalition. "When it comes to the poor they know how to get silent in seven different languages." McDonald's group says ACOG and its sponsors could do more to help house and feed Atlanta's poor.

Supporters of the Olympics say the critics were expecting too much initially and should wait to see the long-term financial impact of hosting the Games.

"Anybody who believes the Olympics is an anti-poverty program is not being realistic," said Bill Campbell, who succeeded Maynard Jackson as mayor. "But anyone with any sense at all will see that the life of virtually everyone in Atlanta will be enhanced tremendously by hosting the Games."

CHAPTER III

Baron of the Rings

BELOW: Jacques Chirac (second from left), then Paris mayor, helps unveil the street sign named for the founder of the modern Olympics. Nelson Pailiou (left), president of the French Olympic committee, and Juan Antonio Samaranch (right), IOC president, look on.

I t is a story most schoolchildren know. For the most part it's still a stirring tale.

19

The Olympic Games were a rite of ancient Greece so powerful and compelling that wars would stop, and gladiators would put aside their swords and shields to duel in naked combat from which all, victors and vanquished alike, could walk away at the end.

Sporting images from the era give us measurements for our modern lives. The discus thrower is our idea of the perfect athlete: Tall, lean, coiled for action. Someone says "marathon," and we think not so much of a town in the hills above the Aegean as the ultimate test of endurance, of going the distance. The crown of laurel is what champions wear. And the best are awarded gold, silver and bronze.

In their rebirth, the Olympics are just as big a force, although the images they evoke now are often less than perfection.

Over the last century, the Games have produced athletes who epitomize the Olympic motto, *Citius, Altius, Fortius*—faster, higher, stronger. Jesse Owens. Jim Thorpe. Paavo Nurmi. Emil Zatopek. Nadia Comaneci. Wilma Rudolph. Mark Spitz. Sonia Henie. Abebe Bikila. Cassius Clay. Edwin Moses. Alberto Juantorena.

They have celebrated the Belle Epoque (Paris, 1900); shown there was more to the American West than just cowboys (St. Louis, 1904); provided diversion from the Great Depression (Lake Placid and Los Angeles, 1932); helped usher in the computer age (Tokyo, 1964), and given an old port a chance to revive by again looking toward the sea (Barcelona, 1992).

The Games have produced dark shadows as well. A showcase for Nazism in Berlin, 1936; dictatorial crackdowns and hundreds of deaths in Mexico City, 1968, and the shock of and overreaction to the black power protests there; terrorism in Munich, 1972, with the Palestinian invasion of the Olympic village wrapping the Olympic rings in a funereal pall; a billion-dollar public debt in Montreal, 1976; East-West boycotts in 1980-84; drugs in 1988.

Still, there is the noble ideal—"The ultimate is not to win, but to take part." These were the words of Pierre de Coubertin, the French baron who created the IOC in 1894.

Nowadays, Coubertin probably would be considered a misguided eccentric. Maybe even a flop. He was a rebel who loved royalty. He was a child of the elite who yearned to educate the masses. His writings were voluminous but largely ignored. A French baron, he took his model of the ideal world from the English and all their empire contained.

But if ever there was a person in the right place at the right time, it was this youngest son of a Parisian hotelier, a short, humorless, unathletic man who became the father of the modern Olympic Games.

In the late 1800s, the buzzword was "internationalism." To be considered truly important, an idea or organization had to be global—or at least known throughout that part of the globe considered to be the center of the world: Europe, northern Africa and the United States. This was the age of steam travel and industrial vitality. Great world's fairs were staged to celebrate mankind's accomplishments, the bigger the better.

Coubertin's vision started on a much smaller scale. He wanted to bring the love of sport and competition that was so much a part of English public schools to France. Coubertin knew of the Cotswold Olympics and the Munch Wenlock Games, revivals of the ancient Olympics held periodically in the English countryside. His ideal laboratory for combining the best educations of the body and the mind was the rough-and-tumble Rugby School of *Tom Brown's School Days*, corporal punishment and all.

His efforts brought a collective yawn from his compatriots. French parents were not keen to have their children pick up the finer points of boxing and soccer. This was a time of arts and letters, not athletics.

But Coubertin's quest was not just to have people run and jump, kick and throw. The spectacle of sport was at least as important to him as the actual competition, and the baron shifted his focus from the grassroots to the grand salons.

Coubertin was a networker a century before his time. In 1892, he tapped his sources to convene a meeting in Paris of politicians, royalty and athletic administrators to discuss the international aspects of sports. At the end of a speech entitled "Physical Exercises in the Modern World," delivered in the grand amphitheater at the Sorbonne, Coubertin referred to the global village just then putting down roots and what role sports could play:

> "It is clear that the telegraph, railroads, the telephone, dedicated research congresses and expositions have done more for peace than all the treaties and diplomatic conventions. Indeed, I expect that athleticism will do even more. ... All this leads to what we should consider the second part of our program. I hope you will help us in the future as you have in the past to pursue this new project. What I mean is that, on a basis conforming to modern life, we re-establish a great and magnificent institution, the Olympic Games."

Others had talked about reviving the Games, which were ended in 394 A.D. by imperial Rome cracking down on pagan rituals, but the talk remained just that. Again, Coubertin's network of contacts kept the issue alive, and the spirit of internationalism gave it added impetus.

Ironically, Coubertin himself felt rebuffed by the initial reaction to his call and moved into the background. "There was total incomprehension," the baron wrote in his memoirs. But rather than drop the idea, he allowed other, more widely known supporters to take the point.

In 1894, back at the Sorbonne, the community we now know as the modern Olympics was born. Borrowing a Latin motto, *Citius, Altius, Fortius*, from the archway of the Jesuit school headed by his close friend, Father Henri Didon, Coubertin convened the first International Athletics Congress.

"Sport is not a luxury," Baron Courcel, president of the congress, said. "It is a necessity. ... Let us bring countries together for friendly sports contests . ... Olympic Games!"

Courcel was a former French ambassador to Germany and one of Coubertin's frontmen. Coubertin himself shared the dais with two other friends, William Sloane of the United States and Charles Herbert of Britain. And by the time the 79 delegates from 13 nations agreed unanimously on June 23, 1894, that the Olympics should be reborn, Coubertin saw his wish come true without having uttered a word to the gathering.

Acting through intermediaries, Coubertin directed the next key items on the agenda.

The Games would be limited to amateurs only (with the exception of professional fencing masters, perhaps the first "Dream Team").

They would be for adults, and only for men. While Coubertin had campaigned vigorously against the spread of anti-Semitism, his liberal leanings did not extend to women's rights, and the Olympics would remain male-only until the 1920s.

The Games would move around. Coubertin felt no single nation or city could afford to become a permanent Olympic stage.

And, as was the case in ancient times, the Olympics would be held every four years.

Paris 1900 was pencilled in as the start of the new Olympic age.

Coubertin wanted the revival to be held in his hometown as part of the Universal Exposition. But almost as soon as the idea was broached, competitors sprang up. There was strong sentiment to have the first Games in Stockholm, a proposal pushed by Sweden's Viktor Balck. So somewhere along the line, Coubertin decided Paris could wait—but Stockholm could, too.

Presenting the idea through Demetrios Bikelas, the delegate from Athens, Coubertin proposed holding the first Games in the Greek capital in 1896. The motion carried unanimously. Suddenly, Athens had a big job on its hands and only two years to get ready.

It wasn't until the final day, in an ornamental garden near what is now the La Defense section of western Paris, that Coubertin had his say. Maintaining his new persona of playing just a minor role, he praised the delegates for their actions.

"It occurred to us to bring together the representatives of international athletics and they, unanimously, have voted for the restitution of a 2,000-year-old idea which, today, as in former ages, stirs the hearts of men," Coubertin said. "Yes, we are rebels. ... And I raise my glass to the Olympic idea, which has crossed the fog of time and returns to shed the light, among us all, of a glow of joyful hope, on the threshold of the 20th century."

Bikelas would become the first president of the International Olympic Committee, and oversee the first modern Games. Coubertin would be the committee's secretary before taking over as president in 1896.

The IOC and the broader Olympic community would ignore, refute and otherwise madden its founder in the years to come. By the time he died in a park in Geneva, Switzerland, in 1937, Coubertin was a bitter man who had little time for his brainchild.

But on an early summer's day in Paris, he was beside himself. His dream had been achieved.

Money Man

If Pierre de Coubertin was the genius behind the modern Olympics, a shy Greek businessman was the banker.

George Averoff did more with his checkbook to make sure the first Games took place and succeeded than all the titled nobility and sports heroes combined.

When Athens was picked to stage the Olympic revival, Greek officials greeted the decision with delight. Then they started looking around at what they had and what was needed, and cringed.

The city was dirty and crowded. Stadiums and arenas were in poor shape and few in number. The Greeks wanted to stage a grand Games but didn't know how to pay for them.

"Athenian expectations were growing daily and hardly at all accorded with reality," Coubertin wrote after a visit to the capital.

Enter Averoff.

Greece had benefitted before from the largesse of its rich son, now living in Alexandria, Egypt. Averoff had quietly financed the construction of three schools in Athens.

Facing a construction bill of 585,000 drachmas (about $65,000 at 1896 exchange rates) for the Olympic stadiums, organizers travelled across the Mediterranean and convinced Averoff to bankroll the project. The actual cost was almost double the estimate; Averoff paid the overruns, too.

Such financial backing allowed Greek organizers to use better materials for the stadiums and pay for related items, such as improved roads, gaslights on the streets, ushers' salaries and even bribes for the city's bureaucrats and underworld.

For his help, Averoff was honored in the way of his ancestors—with a white marble statue. The life-size likeness showed Averoff, with long hair and beard, in modern dress and was placed at the entrance to the new Olympic stadium next to two ancient heads of Hermes, the Greek god of fertility.

After all of this, Averoff became perhaps the most famous Olympic no-show.

Always shy, the Games' greatest philanthropist declined an invitation for some of the best seats in the house at the opening ceremonies and the rest of the first Olympics.

CHAPTER IV

Let the Games Begin

The Olympics came back to life with a flash of pageantry and athletic greatness. They survived by an eyelash.

BELOW: The main stadium of the first modern Olympics peeks from behind a hill in Athens. In the right foreground are the remains of the Temple of Zeus.

ABOVE: The first Olympic champion in more than 1,500 years, James B. Connolly is shown here in 1950. Fifty-four years earlier, he won the hop-step-and-jump at the Athens Games.

Coubertin, the rebellious royalist, found support in Crown Prince Constantine, the Duke of Sparta and son of Greece's King George. A popular figure, Constantine energized the organizing committee and turned public support on the Olympics and other matters to such an extent that Tricoupis resigned. Deligiannes took over as prime minister. The Olympics were saved.

With money from Georges Averoff and other philanthropists, Athens built a gleaming new stadium on the site of the ancient stadium of Herodes Atticus. It was white marble, with steeply banked stands and hairpin turns on the 330-yard, loose-cinder running track. The floor of the stadium was widened from its original dimensions and wooden benches installed on the higher rows, where even round-the-clock construction could not finish the stonework in time for the opening ceremonies.

Other new facilities included a swimming stadium in the port of Piraeus, where the water temperature was 55 degrees; a velodrome brought from Denmark by the crown prince; and tennis courts next to the remains of the Temple of Jupiter, where players still exchange forehands and volleys beneath the towering columns.

Invitations were sent to national athletic leaders to send teams to the Athens Games. Many of these met with sarcasm and derision.

Belgium, Germany and the Netherlands all expressed concern over the principles of amateurism and the ideals of their own sports organizations. Officials in France, Coubertin's homeland, laughed at his idea of subsidizing the first Olympic team. Britain, the baron's idyllic land of sports and scholarship, at first ignored the invitation, in large part because it was sent initially in French and later in German; in the end, the British team consisted of six people, at least two of whom were citizens of other countries.

Perhaps the most noble—and saddest—entry came from Italy. Carlo Aroldi walked from Milan to Athens, a distance of more than 1,000 miles, to get in shape. When he arrived, organizers said he lacked credentials as an amateur and declared him ineligible for Olympic competition.

After Coubertin's committee decided upon Athens as the inaugural host city, Greek officials began to worry that the event was beyond them. Plagued by poor harvests, bad planning, corrupt bureaucrats and the defection of its wealthiest business leaders overseas, Greece was in bad shape.

The government split into two factions, with the anti-Games forces led by a very powerful man—Charilos Tricoupis, the Greek prime minister. Campaigning for the Games was his chief political opponent, Theodoros Deligiannes. For the first time, and even before a race was run, the modern Olympics had encountered government interference. It would not be the last such encounter.

Coubertin and his Greek friend, Bikelas, came to Athens to try to sort things out. They were snubbed by the prime minister, but

In the end, 13 nations sent 311 athletes—all of them male—to Athens for the first modern Olympics, Coubertin's vision of international understanding and peace through sports. Among the delegations was a team from the United States, and that group included the first Olympic champion in more than 1,500 years.

He almost didn't make it to the starting line.

James B. Connolly was a sophomore at Harvard when he read in 1895 that the games of ancient Olympia were to be revived the following year. A star in the hop, step and jump (now known as the triple jump), Connolly asked his school for support and permission to compete in Athens. Harvard promptly told him to get lost. So he went to the Suffolk Athletic Club in south Boston, cut a deal for a uniform and set sail with nine other members of the U.S. team from New York on March 9, 1896, 29 days before the calendar showed the Games were to start.

A pickpocket caught up with Connolly in Naples, Italy, and he was delayed while police investigated; they were unimpressed with his Olympic plans. Barely catching the team's departing train, Connolly and the others made it to Athens on the night of March 25, and found themselves in the midst of a mammoth celebration.

And why not? The Olympic Games were starting the next day!

The Greeks were still living by the Orthodox calendar, which ran 12 days ahead of the Western calendar. It wasn't March 25 at all. It was April 5, and Connolly's event was the first on the opening-day schedule, about 12 hours away.

Only one thing to do, Connolly figured—stay up! Groggy from no sleep after the long journey, Connolly watched as King George opened the Games before an overflow crowd of 100,000 in the Panatheanic Stadium. Then the persistent Crimson sophomore went out and put his competition to bed.

The last of 12 competitors, Connolly was cheered loudly after his first jump by the crew of the *U.S.S. Liberty*, which was docked in Piraeus. "I came quite awake then," Connolly said. He won with a jump of 44 feet, 11 ¾ inches, more than three feet better than runner-up Alexandre Tuffere of France.

He was an Olympic champion, the first since Barasdates, a boxer from Armenia, in 393 A.D.

"It was a moment in a young man's life," Connolly said.

While he was the first person to win a title at the Games in 1,503 years, Connolly was not the first gold medalist. A silver medal went to the winner, and a bronze medal to the runner-up. Gold was considered vulgar, and gold medals—perhaps the ultimate symbol of sports achievement—did not appear until 1904.

With large crowds and close competition, the Games were an athletic success. The United States dominated track and field, then as now the spotlight sport of the Games, winning nine of the 12 events. Greece led the overall medal count with 47 and counted among its 10 champions perhaps the most storied winner of all.

Spiridon Louis looked more like a waiter at a campy

BELOW: Spiridon Louis, who won the first Olympic marathon in 1896, appeared in Greek costume for this 1936 photo.

Greek restaurant than an Olympic champion. The pleats of his traditional skirt and puffy sleeves of his crisp white tunic billowed over knee-high black boots. An embroidered vest complemented the outfit. There was a dark bowl of a cap with a ribbon or crest on his head.

But he was the original marathon man.

The ancient Greeks were no fools. No race in their Games lasted longer than 5,000 meters. Their legends, however, contained the story of the ultimate distance runner, Philippides, who raced to Athens in 449 B.C. with news of victory at Marathon. "Rejoice, we conquer!" he cried. He then dropped dead.

Marathon to Athens is 40 kilometers, or about 23 miles, and organizers decided to restage Philippides' run as the climax to the first modern Games. They hoped a Greek would provide the crowning victory once again.

At Marathon Bridge, 17 runners took off. Edwin Flack, an Australian who lived in London, and Arthur Blake of the United States took the early lead, but eventually caved in to the rigors of the distance. Flack had to be helped off the course after becoming delirious and slugging a fan who came to his aid.

Louis, meanwhile, chugged on.

At the stadium in Athens, the king and 100,000 of his countrymen waited for the winner. Almost three hours after the starting gun at Marathon, word spread that a local hero was in the lead. *"Elleen! Elleen!"* the crowd shouted. "A Greek! A Greek!"

Through the arch and onto the narrow track came Louis, his small frame bathed in dust. The king's sons, George and Constantine, rushed to his side and ran the final lap with him. The crowd went wild as Louis finished the race in 2 hours, 58 minutes, 50 seconds, bowed to the king and was carried off on the shoulders of his fans. The next day, this shepherd who had suddenly become the focus of his nation quietly received his awards—a silver cup, a laurel wreath, an antique vase. He turned down gifts such as a sewing machine and free haircuts.

He accepted a horse and cart. He said he needed them to carry water back home.

The victory by Spiridon Louis in the marathon at Athens ended the first modern Olympics on a very high note. But the tune would soon turn sour.

After the glories of Greece, Paris seemed a fitting spot to continue this new tradition. But the world was changing rapidly. The French capital was caught up in the political and social turmoil of the turn of the century. Coubertin and his fledgling movement could not keep pace.

For the second installment of his sporting spectacle and the staging of it at last in his hometown, Coubertin wanted to build a classic setting—an Olympic Park, containing stadiums and arenas surrounded by Grecian architecture. Paris said no, and elbowed Coubertin aside. It would stage the Games, but in its own way.

It was the beginning of the end of Coubertin's love affair with the modern Olympics, and the start of a long, tough slide for the Games. Instead of the noble stage for athletic endeavor their founder had intended—and which, for the most part, was achieved in Athens—the Olympics became little more than an afterthought wrapped in nationalism.

In 1900 in Paris and 1904 in St. Louis, they were essentially sideshows for world's fairs. Posters for those events depict sporting scenes but make no direct mention of the Olympics. Some athletes in Paris said they were unaware that they had competed in the Games.

The first London Olympics in 1908 were bigger as far as sports were concerned, but an all-British organization from the chairman right down to the competition judges led to disputes over favoritism, especially between the hosts and the United States.

"We have made a hash of our work," Coubertin lamented.

Thank goodness for the athletes.

Take Peggy Abbott, for example. She and her mother were members of the Chicago Golf Club, on vacation in Paris in the summer of 1900. They saw an ad for an international golf tournament and decided to enter. Peggy shot 47 for nine holes to win the contest; her mother

finished seventh. They were Olympians and never knew it.

Such disorganization helped women to participate, even if in very small members. Of 1,330 athletes from 22 nations in Paris, 11 competitors were women. That included Charlotte Cooper of Britain, who won the Olympic tennis tournament the same summer she won Wimbledon.

Soccer joined the Olympic program, as did cricket, croquet and rugby. Track and field was staged on the grass in the Bois de Boulogne, where trees often got in the way of javelins. And the biggest winner was an American who had to overcome religious controversy and an angry teammate's fists.

Alvin Kranzlein was the world's best hurdler. He came to Paris favored in the 110-meter and 200-meter hurdles and the 60-meter dash. He won all three, but it was his record-setting fourth title that made him part of Olympic lore.

Because organizers feared poor attendance and worse if they held big events on Bastille Day, the long jump final was moved back a day—to Sunday, July 15. Most of the U.S. track and field athletes came from universities with rules against competing on the Christian Sabbath. That included Meyer Prinstein, a Jewish student from Syracuse and world record-holder in the long jump. Kranzlein, a Christian, went to Penn, which said its athletes could compete on Sunday if they so chose. Kranzlein jumped and won, soaring 23 feet, 6 ¾ inches and beating Prinstein's mark from the preliminaries by a half-inch.

Prinstein was infuriated. He ran up to Kranzlein and challenged him to a jump-off the next day. Kranzlein refused. So Prinstein started punching Kranzlein, before other members of the U.S. team broke up the fight.

Kranzlein retired from track that year but Prinstein kept competing and got his Olympic title in 1904, in St. Louis.

Coubertin wanted to bring the Games to America because U.S. athletes had been such enthusiastic supporters and overwhelming winners in Athens and Paris. It was hard to sell his idea to Americans.

Coubertin and William Sloane, an influential professor at Princeton, had hoped New York would be the first U.S. Olympic host. When the Big Apple reacted to that suggestion with the indifference it often gives to out-of-towners, Coubertin and Sloane approached Chicago. The city by Lake Michigan agreed, but another Midwestern boomtown butted in.

The American West, long the province of only the most daring or outcast, was opening up. Trains and riverboats finally gave average people the chance to invade the vast prairies and rich mountain ranges. And St. Louis was the gateway to this bounty.

It was staging a world's fair, the Louisiana Purchase Exhibition, in 1904, and thought it would be a nice touch to include a little sports, maybe something like the Olympics. Coubertin hesitated, but—as successors would find out later for themselves—he hadn't bargained on the power of the White House. President Theodore Roosevelt sided with St. Louis and the Olympics were moved to the banks of the Mississippi.

It was a terrible mistake.

For reasons ranging from the Russo-Japanese War to lingering hard feelings from the Louisiana Purchase 101 years before, foreign athletes snubbed the St. Louis Games. Only 12 nations sent teams, and of the 687 athletes entered, 525 were from the United States.

Needless to say, it turned into a star-spangled show, if not a well-organized one. These were two-fisted games, with boxing—even women's boxing—on the program. Baseball, lacrosse and water polo appeared, with the latter labeled "softball in the water" by the disgruntled German team.

George Poage of Milwaukee became the first black to win an Olympic medal, finishing third in the 400-meter hurdles. But the appearances of two other black athletes represented the kind of carnival quality that draped itself over the third Olympics like the smell of stale cotton candy.

The world's fair included an exhibit on the Boer War, and two Zulu tribesmen—Lentauw and Yamasani—were imported. They ran in

ABOVE: The winner of perhaps the most famous Olympic marathon, Johnny Hayes, as he appeared at the 1908 Games (left) and later in his career as a food broker.

the marathon, wearing bib numbers 35 and 36, and became the first black Africans to compete in the Olympics.

Coubertin stayed away from all of this. He never left Paris, disgusted by reports of "pygmy Olympics" and plans to stage tobacco-spitting contests.

Rome was supposed to stage the next Games but pulled out for financial reasons. Coubertin hoped that moving the Olympics to his beloved London would have better results. His hopes were shattered.

Britain prides itself on a reputation for sportsmanship and fair play. But it also is a nation of iconoclasts, and that was never more evident than at the 1908 Olympics.

Believing that events such as Wimbledon, the Henley Regatta and horse-racing's Derby gave Britain nonpareil expertise in running top sports events, the IOC allowed the British to control the Games from top to bottom. The Games were, indeed, well-organized and widely promoted. They attracted the largest field thus far, 2,035 athletes from 22 nations. Although part of a world's fair, the Franco-British Exposition, they retained their own identity.

But that identity was British from beginning to end.

First, the hosts refused to fly the Irish flag. Then, when competition started, British judges and referees blatantly favored British athletes, leading to formal protests from at least five countries, loudest and longest from the United States. British athletes won 56 gold medals—which were awarded for the first time—and 145 overall, more than double the totals for the second-place Americans.

The protests were so widespread that the British organizers issued an official document, "Replies to Criticism of the Olympic Games."

And the IOC made sure that it never again allowed one nation to manage so many parts of the Games.

The next Olympics in 1912 would mark 20 years since Coubertin first called for a revival of the Games. The modern version now appeared to be in great need of its own resuscitation. Fortunately, it found the perfect location—and the perfect athlete—to do just that.

The Runner Stumbles

Search the list of winners of the Olympic marathon and you won't find the name of perhaps the most famous Olympic marathon runner of all.

Dorando Pietri was a small man from a tiny village near Modena, Italy. The weather on the day of the marathon at the London Olympics was ideal for him—hot and humid. Starting at Windsor Castle 26 miles west of the city, the field took a fast early pace, knocking out runners by the block. At the 18-mile mark, it seemed certain that only Pietri or Charles Hefferon of South Africa could win.

But Hefferon made a tragic mistake that seems unbelievable in this day. Two miles from the finish line at White City Stadium, Hefferon accepted a glass of champagne from a fan. He soon became dizzy, and Pietri—after first charging too fast after his staggering adversary—finally passed the South African a half-mile from the stadium entrance.

The nearest runner to Pietri was John Hayes, a 22-year-old sporting-goods sales clerk at Bloomingdale's in New York. The British crowd, in a notoriously anti-American mood all during the Games, cheered wildly as an Italian runner entered the stadium first. If a Brit couldn't win, they figured, let it be anyone but a Yank.

Their cheering started one lap too soon. They could not have imagined what would happen next.

The heat finally got to Pietri with a single 385-yard circuit of the stadium track to go. First, he turned the wrong way as he exited the tunnel. Finally pointed in the right direction, he stumbled exhausted to the track. British officials ran to his side, but Pietri waved them off, knowing he would be disqualified if they touched him.

He rose, ran a few steps, then stumbled a second time. This time the officials ignored his protests. Over and over they helped Pietri to his feet, until they saw Hayes enter the stadium, gaining steadily on the collapsed leader.

The crowd of 68,000 was going wild. So the officials picked up Pietri and carried him across the finish line, then ordered the Italian flag raised in victory.

"It was impossible to leave him there," the official report said of the unorthodox assistance, "for it looked as if he might die in the very presence of the Queen."

Hayes and the Americans did not hold with such royal privilege. Their protest was upheld and Hayes was declared the winner in 2 hours, 55 minutes, 18.4 seconds, almost three-quarters of a second slower than Pietri's official-assisted time.

Dorando came back to the stadium the next day to receive a special gold cup from Queen Alexandra and complain that he could have won the race on his own if the officials had kept their hands off.

Maybe. Maybe not. Photos from that day show Dorando lying on the track in a trancelike state short of the finish line, unable to crawl, let alone run.

Despite his failure, Dorando became a worldwide celebrity. Songwriters, including an up-and-coming American named Irving Berlin, set his saga to music. In those politically incorrect days, Berlin's offering was entitled, "Dorando He'sa Gooda for Not."

CHAPTER V

Jim Thorpe

BELOW: Jim Thorpe displays the athletic form that helped him win the 1912 Olympic decathlon and the title of World's Greatest Athlete.

He did not look like superman. He hardly looked like an athlete.

31

ABOVE: The decathlon did not display all of Jim Thorpe's skills. He was also an All-America football player at Carlisle Indian School.

You would glance at Jim Thorpe and think, "How did this truck driver invade the Olympics?"

But the looks of a laborer belied Thorpe's athletic powers. He was the greatest competitor of his time, and he helped save the Olympics before being ostracized for 70 years, a banishment that would help lead to his early death.

Thorpe was an American original. A member of the Sac and Fox tribe born in Shawnee, Oklahoma, in 1888, Thorpe was raised at an Indian school in Carlisle, Pennsylvania, where he honed his speed, strength and agility to an incredible degree. He came to the peak of his ability just as the Olympics was most in need of a superstar. After the debacles of the early 1900s,

Coubertin and his followers faced a key moment in 1912.

As it has uncannily done throughout its history, the IOC turned at the right moment to the right place. It picked Stockholm, Sweden, to host the fifth Games and found there two elements unknown to the Olympics before and vital to their survival—government cooperation and impeccable organization.

The Swedes jumped on the Olympic bandwagon. They built a 30,000-seat stadium and a new swimming arena, and festooned their capital city with flags and banners. It was like an Olympics in the midst of a country fair, and this time the Games were the main attraction.

And the biggest star was Thorpe.

At Carlisle, Thorpe excelled in baseball, track and football, scoring all the points for his unknown school in an 18-15 upset of mighty Harvard in 1911. The following year, he ran 97 yards for a touchdown against Army and was named to the All-America team for the second consecutive season.

Thorpe won letters in 11 sports. He was the intercollegiate ballroom dancing champion of 1911. And his versatility made him close to a one-man U.S. track team in Stockholm, where he entered four events—the high jump, the long jump, the pentathlon and the ultimate test, the decathlon.

Thorpe came in fourth in the high jump and seventh in the long jump. In the multi-events, however, he couldn't be touched.

At that time, the pentathlon was a track event—long jump, javelin, discus and runs of 200 and 1,500 meters. Thorpe won easily, finishing first in the long jump, discus and the two runs and taking a third in the javelin.

The decathlon was infrequently contested at that time; in fact, Thorpe never had entered one until he got to Stockholm. What he did there, however, set a standard for years to come. When the first of the decathlon's three days ended, Thorpe had a comfortable lead and never looked back. He won four events (shot put, high jump, discus and 110-meter hurdles), finished second in two others (100 meters and 1,500) and totaled 8,412 points, 998 more than the old world record and 688 better than Hugo Wieslander, Sweden's silver medalist.

Among the also-rans in the decathlon and pentathlon was Avery Brundage, a U.S. teammate who would play a major role in a later, darker part of Thorpe's life.

The world went wild for Thorpe. In addition to his gold medals, he received a chalice covered in jewels from Russia's Czar Nicholas and a bronze bust of Sweden's King Gustav V. The bust was presented by the king himself, who came right to the point.

"Sir," said the monarch, "you are the greatest athlete in the world."

To which the commoner replied: "Thanks, king."

Back home, a tickertape parade down Broadway greeted the new American hero.

"I heard people yelling my name," Thorpe would recall, "and I couldn't realize how one fellow could have so many friends."

Some turned out to be fair-weather friends. Storm clouds were gathering for the man whose Indian name was Wa-Tho-Huck, or "Bright Path."

Back before he was a well-known star, Thorpe played baseball for a minor league team in North Carolina. He was paid $25 a week. That made him a professional, and that made him ineligible to compete in the Olympics.

When word of this came out in early 1913, America's Olympic leaders were scandalized. They demanded an explanation. Thorpe responded with the truth.

"I hope I will be partly excused by the fact that I

BELOW: Jim Thorpe, in football uniform, greets fellow American Indians in this 1926 photo.

was simply an Indian schoolboy and did not know all about such things," he wrote to James E. Sullivan, chairman of the Amateur Athletic Union. "In fact, I did not know I was doing wrong because I was doing what I knew several other college men had done except that they did not use their own names."

Thorpe was not being disingenuous in this matter. College stars long had preserved their amateur eligibility and made good money by playing professionally under assumed names, and the practice didn't stop once Thorpe was caught. Perhaps the most famous of these pseudonym stars was John McNally, "the vagabond halfback" at Notre Dame in the 1920s, who played at the same time for the Green Bay Packers as Johnny Blood. He picked that name from the marquee of a movie theater showing *Blood and Sand*, starring Rudolph Valentino.

ABOVE: After losing his Olympic medals in a dispute over amateurism, Jim Thorpe often had to scramble to make ends meet. One of his jobs: laborer on the construction site of the Los Angeles County Hospital.

Right: Olympic champion Jim Thorpe, in full American Indian outfit.

In his letter to Sullivan, Thorpe noted that he had turned down "offers amounting to thousands of dollars since my victories … because I did not care to make money from my athletic skills." He said he hoped the AAU "and the people will not be too hard in judging me."

The feeling on the streets was that Thorpe should be exonerated. But in the paneled clubrooms where Olympic sports were governed, there was little sympathy. The AAU and the American Olympic Committee came down hard, striking his name from all record books and apologizing for including him on the Olympic team. The IOC asked that Thorpe's medals and trophies be returned. It kept them locked in a vault for more than seven decades, even while Brundage, his old teammate, served as committee president from 1952-72.

Thorpe played professional baseball and football until 1928, but when the Depression hit, his luck ran out. He dug ditches, worked as a movie extra and even as a bouncer at a bar. He sold the movie rights to his life story to MGM for $1,500, and had to be admitted to a hospital as a charity case when he developed cancer in 1951. Two years later, the man voted the greatest athlete of the first half of the 20th century in an Associated Press poll died of a heart attack. He was buried in Mauch Chunk, Pennyslvania, a down-at-the-heels town in the Pocono Mountains with no connection to the fabled star expect that it agreed to change its name to Jim Thorpe, Pennsylvania, if it could have his body as a tourist attraction.

While Thorpe's fortunes failed, the Olympics thrived. The tousle-haired Indian from Oklahoma had not done it alone, but his heroics in Stockholm helped focus world attention on the sports festival and created interest that was sustained through the coming years of war. Periodic campaigns to rehabilitate his memory rose and fell, but finally—with professional athletes in all sports knocking on the Olympic doors—the IOC said it was wrong. It reinstated Thorpe

Top: Forty years after he helped to take Jim Thorpe's Olympic medals away, then-IOC President Avery Brundage, right, shakes hands with Thorpe at a fund-raising telethon.

Above: IOC President Juan Antonio Samaranch, with two of the late Jim Thorpe's children, at a ceremony in 1983 when Thorpe's two Olympic gold medals were returned to his family.

as an Olympic champion and returned his medals to his children.

One memento of the days when the Bright Path shone stayed with the committee. It was the bejeweled bowl from the czar, an ornate silver cauldron given to the greatest athlete of his time. It sits in a place of honor in the Olympic Museum in Lausanne, Switzerland.

CHAPTER VI

Between the Wars

ABOVE: The U.S. team for the 1924 Winter Olympics parades into the stadium at Chamonix.

BELOW: Teams file into the stadium at Antwerp for the start of the 1920 Olympics.

Y ou cannot separate the Olympics from war.

BELOW: Many sports have come and gone from the Olympic schedule. Even rugby, with the American team shown here, had a shot at gold-medal glory.

ABOVE: Plenty of good seats available for the opening ceremonies of the 1924 Games in Paris.

The Greek city-states used to put down their arms for the ancient games, their warriors battling instead in naked glory on the running track or the wrestling mat. It was, indeed, an Olympic truce.

Times—and wars—had changed by the early 20th century. Conflicts spread over entire continents and beyond, and rendered even the thought of international athletic competition meaningless.

The Olympics stopped for the two world wars. But the success of the 1912 Games in Stockholm meant a return after World War I was inevitable. And staging the 1936 Games in Berlin—while debatable in timing—allowed the world to glimpse the evil that would turn into the thunder and lightning of World War II.

Berlin, in fact, was supposed to host the Games in 1916, but the "War to End Wars" was raging. Peace found many of the heroes of Stockholm dead on the battlefields, and led the IOC to place the 1920 Games in Antwerp, Belgium, a country that perhaps suffered more than any other during the fighting.

Organizers had 20 months to put the Games together, and did so with ease. Antwerp donated a flag, a big white banner with the five Olympic rings in the center and a golden fringe around the edge, that is still handed down from host city to host city. A 30,000-seat stadium—it was rarely full, despite ticket

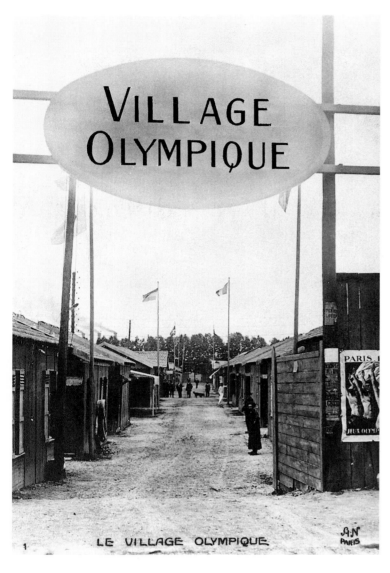

ABOVE: The entrance to the Olympic Village in Paris, 1924. Note the crude huts and the total lack of visible security measures.

RIGHT: Sonja Heine skates with men's world champion Gilles Grafton at the 1924 Winter Games in Chamonix, France.

prices of around 30 cents—was built and a requiem Mass was held for the war dead.

Germany, Austria, Hungary, Bulgaria and Turkey—the defeated powers of World War I—were not invited to the Olympics.

A survivor of the war was among the heroes of the Games.

Joseph Guillemot was a soldier in the French army during the war when his unit was hit by mustard gas. The poison ripped into his lungs and left them badly scarred. But the 5-foot-3 Guillemot was able to recover and won the 5,000 meters over one of the great names of track, Paavo Nurmi, by 30 yards. It was Nurmi's only loss at Antwerp—he won the 10,000 meters plus golds in the team and individual cross-country races—and his lone Olympic loss to anyone other than a Finnish teammate.

Nurmi was not the first of the "Flying Finns." That honor went to his idol, Hannes Kolehmainen, who won three golds in Stockholm and returned to win the Antwerp

marathon by just 70 yards, the closest finish in the history of the Olympic race.

Another big winner from Stockholm who returned with honors eight years later was an American swimmer whose name would eventually become synonymous with another sport—surfing.

Duke Kahanamoku was a son of Hawaiian royalty, but duke was not his title. That was his first name, chosen because the Duke of Edinburgh was a visitor to the palace in Honolulu the day he was born. In the pool, he was king, setting a world record in the 100-meter freestyle in Stockholm and winning the 100 and 800 freestyles in Antwerp. One of the world's biggest surfing championships, the Duke Kahanamoku Classic on Maui, is named in his honor.

When the Antwerp Games closed on an austere but peaceful note, Coubertin reminded that world that "these festivals are, above all, the festivals of human unity." The next few editions would underscore both how strong that unity could be, and how fragile.

The Olympics were now part of the world's calendar, and they were expanding. When war threatened in 1915, Coubertin moved his home—and, thus, the IOC's headquarters—to the lakefront city of Lausanne, Switzerland, to take advantage of Swiss neutrality.

Maybe it was the sight of Mont Blanc rising across the lake, or the success of figure skating and ice hockey on the schedule at Antwerp. For whatever reason, the IOC recognized the growing popularity of winter sports, and in 1924 added a Winter Games to the Olympic schedule.

These were to be held in the same country as the Summer Games. So, with Paris set for its second round of Olympic hosting that year, the inaugural Winter Olympics were staged in Chamonix, France. Canada won the ice hockey gold medal, while figure skating titles went to Herma Plank-Szabo of Austria and Sweden's Gillis Grafstroem, the winner in Antwerp.

Chamonix was plagued by a cycle of freeze and thaw that winter, and bad weather persisted in Paris as the Summer Games approached. The River Seine flooded and, together with a shaky French economy,

threatened to force the Olympics to be moved to Los Angeles. Eventually the river returned to its banks, the franc steadied and the City of Lights staged a memorable Games.

Interest among nations, athletes and spectators reached new heights. With the world in a peaceful lull, a record 45 nations sent 3,092 athletes to Paris, and fans were so eager to see them that scalpers appeared on the Olympic scene for the first time. Tickets for the opening ceremonies May 4 sold on the street for up to three times their face value.

The Paris Games were headlined by some old stars—Nurmi and Kahanamoku—and some new ones—American swimmer Johnny Weissmuller and a rower on the U.S. eights, Benjamin Spock. Weissmuller would go on to become Tarzan in the movies; Spock, the No. 7 oarsman on that gold-medal crew, would become an internationally known authority on child care.

But most people know the '24 Games for a lilting theme song, for young lads running on a Scottish beach, for the goodness and fair play of two British rivals. Thanks to *Chariots of Fire*, the 1981 Oscar winner for best picture, the deeds of Harold Abrahams and Eric Liddell became common knowledge a mere 57 years after they occurred.

Some of the film's drama is the work of screenwriters and history benders. But these facts remain, and they are just as appealing as the Hollywood glitz:

Abrahams was the son of a Lithuanian Jew, educated at Cambridge, a lawyer in the making. He was relentless in his quest to become the first European winner of the Olympic 100 meters.

Liddell was the son of missionaries from Scotland. He was the Commonwealth record-holder in the 100-yard dash and one of the few people who could challenge Abrahams in the short sprints. A devout Christian, he refused to run on Sundays.

As the film showed, the Olympic 100-meter heats were set for a Sunday. Abrahams ran. Liddell did not, instead seeking out a Scottish church in Paris and preaching the sermon.

Abrahams went on to win the 100 in 10.6 seconds on July 7, beating favored Americans

ABOVE: Eric Liddell, the divinity student from Scotland who won the 400-meter gold medal in 1924. His triumph and rivalry with teammate Harold Abrahams were immortalized in the film, "Chariots of Fire."

Charley Paddock and Jackson Scholz. Liddell, in his unorthodox style of running with head thrown back and arms flailing, won the 400 meters and took the bronze in the 200, where Abrahams finished sixth.

Liddell followed his parents into missionary work in China and died of a brain tumor in a Japanese internment camp in World War II. Abrahams became a wealthy businessman, writer and radio commentator in London.

Neither of them competed in the Olympics again.

"Liddell turned to the 400 meters mainly because he was not willing to run in the 100 meters, which was on a Sunday," Abrahams wrote years later. "Eric broke every possible rule of style, with his head right back, knees well up and arms all over the place. But, my goodness, what spiritual power."

As for his own feat, Abrahams said: "I am still amazed at the enormous difference to my life that 10 seconds or so on the evening of July 7, 1924, made."

Another British athlete on whom a character in *Chariots of Fire* was loosely based became a star in the next Games, in Amsterdam in 1928. David Lord Burghley, a future member of Parliament, won the 400-meter hurdles in an Olympic-record 53.4 seconds. Men were joined on the track by women for the first time in Amsterdam, and among them was a Canadian star with one of the most enchanting nicknames you could find.

Ethel Catherwood was "The Saskatoon Lily," breezing in from the northern plains to win the high jump.

So the Roaring 20s ended with the Olympics roaring right along with the rest of the Jazz Age. But like the rest of the world, the Games were about to enter a decade that would change them forever.

Storm Clouds

ABOVE: Britain's Lord Burghley takes the baton from a teammate in the 400-meter relays at the 1932 Games.

BELOW: Action in the 1,600-meter relay atthe 1932 Games in Los Angeles. The United States won the race in a world-record 8 minutes, 8.2 seconds.

I t was a time of soup kitchens and boarded-up factories. Wall Street had collapsed. The great breadbasket of the Midwest had turned into a Dust Bowl.

ABOVE: The unusual finish of U.S. sprinter Charlie Paddock is shown in this 1931 picture.

BELOW: Babe Didriksen Zaharias clears the hurdle in a 1932 meet. She wears the uniform of Employees Casualty insurance company, which she led to the national team championship.

As the Depression gripped the nation and much of the rest of the world, more and more people decided to seek their fortune in that almost mythical land of milk and honey—California.

So why shouldn't the Olympics give it a try, too?

Back in the Roaring 20s, when the IOC awarded LA the Games for 1932, prosperity was the key word. The Los Angeles Olympics would signal a new, expansion stage in the revival of the sports festival, the IOC believed, with more athletes from more nations competing that ever before.

But then came the stock market crash of 1929, and the world's economy was in a shambles. The Winter Olympics in Lake Placid, New York, took a beating, with only 307 athletes from 17 countries able to attend, and as the start of the Summer Games approached in July 1932 the list of regrets grew ominously long, with 20 nations eventually replying that they could not afford to send teams.

Nations with teetering economies and fans with empty wallets suddenly placed Olympic

participation very low on their list of priorities. A Norwegian living in Los Angeles had to pay for his home country's team to attend. Even the host U.S. team suffered, raising just about half of the $350,000 needed to field a full squad for Los Angeles.

It took a Southern California real estate magnate to save the day. William May Garland was president of the Los Angeles Olympic Organizing Committee and was able to raise enough money through business and government grants to lure 1,400 athletes from 37 nations—still the lowest number of Olympians in more than 25 years.

Garland's business sense and knowledge of housing trends did produce two unique legacies for Los Angeles:

In the hills south of the city, Garland built the first Olympic Village. It was a big oval of 550 wood frame and stucco cottages, and all of the male athletes were to be housed there. Until this time, teams had made up their own Olympic accommodations, usually in hotels or private homes, and didn't mingle much away from the competition. When Garland unveiled

ABOVE: Babe Didriksen Zaharias, far right, on her way to a world-record 11.8 seconds in a heat of the women's 80-meter hurdles at the 1932 Games.

BELOW: Duke Kahanamoku, son of Hawaiian royalty, who won three Olympic swimming gold medals in 1912 and 1920.

45

ABOVE: Paavo Nurmi of Finland leads American Mel Dalton over the water jump in the Olympic steeplechase in 1928.

his idea for a common village—complete with fire department, hospital and post office—many athletes and coaches screamed that they could not live so close to their rivals and still get ready for competition. But once they tried it, Olympians loved the village. A spirit of camaraderie enveloped the community and it became an essential part of the Olympic scene. Ask just about any Olympic athlete today what his or her lasting memory is from the Games, and chances are they will say, "Living in the village."

Once the Games were over, Garland dismantled the village homes and sold them for low-cost housing, and the money raised

helped the Los Angeles Games turn a profit—the first ever from Olympic competition.

There were innovations in the stadiums, too, most notably electronic timing for track. It came in handy in the men's 100 meters, where American Ralph Metcalfe appeared to edge teammate Eddie Tolan for the gold medal. Judges, however, reviewed the photo finish films and declared Tolan the winner by two inches.

In these American games, U.S. athletes were the unrivaled stars.

In addition to Tolan, there was Mildred "Babe" Didrikson, an all-around athlete from Texas who won gold medals in the javelin and 80-meter hurdles. She might have added a third gold, in the high jump, but judges ruled that her Western roll violated rules against diving over the bar and gave the title instead to teammate Jean Shirley.

Helene Madison took the women's 100- and 200-meter freestyle swimming golds and anchored the American women's 400-meter freestyle relay team to a world-record 4:38, cutting almost 10 seconds off the previous mark.

The biggest star of the Games was another American swimmer. Clarence "Buster" Crabbe was a 24-year-old law student at the University of Southern California and the best freestyle swimmer in the country. The best freestyler in the world was a Frenchman, Jean Taris, and they were meet in a memorable duel in the 400-meter race in Los Angeles.

One of a trio of swift Japanese swimmers, Takashi Yokoyama, lowered the Olympic record to 4:51.4 in qualifying rounds, still well off Taris' world mark of 4:47. But the Japanese challengers were never threats in the final, where Taris went to the front and held a two-length lead at 200 meters. Crabbe closed the gap to a length with 100 meters to go and caught Taris halfway through the final stretch. The 10,000 fans—including 1924 400-freestyle champion Johnny Weissmuller—jumped to their feet, yelling loudly for Crabbe to get the gold. Weissmuller even climbed a fence to get closer to the pool for a better look. As Crabbe touched the wall, he looked up and saw Taris' head bob, a sure sign the Frenchman had just come in No. 2. Crabbe was the gold-medalist in 4:48.4, to Taris' 4:48.5.

"That one-tenth of a second changed my life," Crabbe would remember years later. The gold medal attracted Paramount Pictures, which signed Crabbe to a $200-a-week movie contract—even though he had never acted before. Paramount was looking for a big, strong, good-looking athlete to compete in action pictures against Weissmuller, who jumped from his Olympic gold medals to a long-running role as Tarzan at MGM. Crabbe's first feature at Paramount was *King of the Jungle*, in which he played Kaspa, the Lion Man. He would later fill such roles as space pilot Buck Rogers, Western outlaw Billy the Kid—and even one film as Weissmuller's successor as Tarzan.

Despite the bad economic climate and low athlete turnout, the Los Angeles Games were a sporting and financial success. They also were among the most open in terms of diverse racial and ethnic backgrounds. Crabbe, for instance, was part Polynesian. Japanese athletes gave their first impressive performances in swimming and gymnastics. And Tolan—who wore eyeglasses and chewed gum as he ran—became the first black athlete to win an Olympic sprint title with his narrow victory over Metcalfe.

ABOVE: Before he was Tarzan, Johnny Weissmuller was an Olympic swimming star, winning five gold medals and setting more than 50 world records.

BELOW LEFT: Two U.S. swimming stars, Johnny Weissmuller, left, and Duke Kahanamoku, chat at the 1924 Games in Paris.

ABOVE: The Olympic flame is
flanked by hundreds of Nazi
Youth and surrounded by
swastikas at the opening
ceremonies of the 1936 Berlin
Games.

Such changes would be even more evident at the next Summer Games, where race, not races, became the primary issue.

When the Olympics come to town, the pomp and ceremony can usually be counted upon to overshadow all else. But in Berlin in 1936, the five rings were almost overwhelmed by the swastika of Nazi Germany.

Adolf Hitler was looking for a stage from which to promulgate his beliefs of Aryan superiority. The Olympics, awarded to the German capital in 1931, before the Third Reich came to power, gave him the ultimate platform. Jewish groups in the United States protested and called for a boycott of the Games, and U.S. Olympic officials finally approved sending a team by a narrow 58-56 vote.

Plans were made to stage a "Peoples Olympics" in Barcelona, but those preparations ended with the outbreak of the Spanish Civil War.

Heeding the advice of a group of members led by Avery Brundage of the United States to leave politics alone, the IOC decided to keep the Games in Berlin and a watchful eye on the Fuhrer. It also extracted from him a promise that the Berlin Olympics would be free of racial discrimination.

That pledge, the IOC said, meant that Jewish athletes should be part of the German team. Hitler was appalled and told IOC president Henri de Baillet-Latour: "When you are invited to a friend's home, you don't tell him how to run it, do you?"

Baillet-Latour's responses was quick and to the point: "Excuse me, Mr. Chancellor, when the five rings are raised over the stadium, it is no longer Germany. It is the Olympics, and we are masters here."

The German team for the Summer Games did include one Jewish member, fencer Helene Mayer, the women's foil gold medalist in 1928 who had moved to the United States to teach German at a California college. Mayer took the silver this time behind another Jewish athlete, Ilona Schacherer of Hungary. On the medal stand, Mayer gave the Nazi salute of "Heil, Hitler" and was applauded by the crowd.

Hitler made no attempt to hide his desire to use the Olympics for propaganda. The 70,000-seat Reichssportfeld and surrounding arenas in a huge park to the west of the capital's downtown were constructed in heroic style—huge columns, vast plazas and arcades. All were festooned with the black swastika and iron cross of Hitler's domain.

In case anyone missed the point, the Fuhrer preceded the Games with propaganda bulletins, sent in 14 languages to 3,000 newspapers and magazines around the world. These contained tracts on the superiority of the Aryan civilization, the evils of Jews and the ultimate inferiority of blacks.

"The Americans ought to be ashamed of themselves for letting their medals be won by Negroes," Hitler wrote in one of the bulletins. "I myself would never shake hands with one of them."

His propaganda minister, Joseph Goebbels, referred to black athletes as "auxiliaries" and deducted their gold, silver and bronze from the medal charts.

The Games opened with the Olympic flame carried into the stadium before rows and rows of brown-shirted soldiers and Hitler Youth, their right arms extended in salute. The Fuhrer sat in the chancellor's box and those who passed were told to shout "Sieg Heil." The American team did not salute at all. The crowd jeered them.

The competition opened with the shot put, and Hitler could not have been more pleased by the outcome. Winning the gold medal was Hans Woellke, a German policeman. Hitler presided at the medals ceremonies and shook the winner's hand.

But things were much different later that day when

BELOW: Bands from 46 German military units mass on the infield of the Berlin Olympic stadium during opening ceremonies.

the high jump was decided. Cornelius Johnson won the gold medal with an Olympic-record leap of 6 feet, 8 inches. The silver went to teammate David Albritton, at 6-6 ¾. Both Johnson and Albritton were black. The best German jumper, Gustav Weinkoetz, finished in a four-way tie for sixth.

Hitler watched the competition, but left the stadium before the medals were awarded.

Throughout the Games, the clouds of racial bias and the approaching war cast a chill shadow. Black athletes continued to be ignored by top officials. Two Jewish members of the American team, Marty Glickman and Sam Stoller, were yanked from the 400-meter relay race, bringing charges of anti-Semitism. And a Korean runner, Sohn Kee Chung, won the marathon but was denied the honor of collecting the gold medal under either his own

ABOVE RIGHT: Leni Riefenstahl helps edit the soundtrack for her film on the 1936 Olympics. The movie was a major part of Hitler's propoganda use of the Games, but it also is recognized as a screen classic for its cinematography.

BELOW: Jesse Owens soars to victory in the long jump, one of four Olympic gold medals he won in 1936. Hitler repeatedly snubbed the American star.

flag or his own name. Japan occupied Korea, and Sohn was entered as Kitei Son, the Japanese version of his name. He won the marathon in 2:29.19.2, more than two minutes faster than Ernie Harper of Britain. Another Korean, Nam Sung Yong, was third.

On the victory stand, the medals were awarded and the Japanese national anthem was played. Sohn and Nam lowered their heads as the white flag with the red Rising Sun was raised. "It was unendurable, humiliating torture," Sohn said. "I hadn't run for Japan. I ran for myself and my oppressed Korean people. I could not prevent myself from crying. I wished I had never come to Berlin."

When the South Korean capital of Seoul hosted the Olympics in 1988, the Olympic flame was carried by Sohn on the final lap.

From all the tumult of Berlin, however, the enduring image is of one athlete eclipsing the politics and the hate mongering by doing what he did best. He ran faster and jumped farther than anyone else.

He was an American, a black man. His name was Jesse Owens.

James Cleveland Owens was the son of a cotton picker and the grandson of slaves, born September 12, 1913, in Danville, Alabama. His

LEFT: U.S. teammates Jesse Owens, left, and Frank Wykoff work out in the Olympic Village in Berlin.

BELOW: After his fame as an Olympic champion faded, Jesse Owens was forced into stunts, such as running against race horses, as he did here in 1948 at Bay Meadows.

ABOVE: The 200-meter Olympic record falls as Jesse Owens easily wins his heat in 21.1 seconds. Owens won the 100, 200 and long jump, and led the U.S. 400-meter relay to victory.

family called him J.C., and that got slurred into Jesse, and that name stuck.

When Owens was 9, his family moved to Cleveland, Ohio, where he set national high school records in the 100- and 200-yard dashes and the long jump. He won a track scholarship to Ohio State, and there became the best-known sprinter in the country. At the Big Ten championships in Ann Arbor, Michigan, in 1935, Owens turned in perhaps the most incredible 45 minutes ever seen in a track meet. Between 3:15 p.m. and 4 p.m., he set five world records and tied a sixth—in the 100-yard dash, the long jump, the 220-yard dash, the 200-meters, the 220-yard hurdles and the 200-meter hurdles. He went to Berlin the following year as the favorite to win the long jump, 100- and 200-meters, and thus set up a direct confrontation for the racial theories of the host.

The assault started with the 100. Owens and Metcalfe, the 1932 silver medalist, shared the world record of 10.2 seconds and dominated the heats. In the final, Owens took the lead out of the blocks and beat Metcalfe by a yard in 10.3 seconds.

Next for Owens came the long jump—and unexpected help from one of Hitler's favorites.

Luz Long was a blue-eyed blond from Germany who was one of the few athletes given a chance of beating Owens. The world record was 26 feet, 8 ¼ inches, set by Owens in that incredible three-quarters of an hour at Michigan the previous year, and no one else in the world was coming close. But as Owens arrived at the Olympic pit, he saw Long landing practice jumps in the 26-foot range. A bit unnerved by this, Owens—still in his warmup suit—went to test the runway and landed in the sand. The German officials counted this as a jump, leaving him just two leaps to qualify for the final. On his second jump, Owens fouled. Just one try remained for the world record-holder to reach the qualifying mark of 23-5 ½ and make the final.

What happened next has turned into Olympic legend.

Long may have looked the part of the Aryan hero, but he had no time for such beliefs. He saw a competitor struggling and offered some advice. "You could qualify with your eyes closed," he told Owens. Then he suggested that Owens place his takeoff mark several inches behind the foul line, to avoid accidental elimination. Owens took the hint and easily qualified.

The final rounds were that afternoon. With Hitler watching, Owens set an Olympic record of 25 5-½ on his first jump and extended that to 25-10 a short while later. Long matched that mark on his next-to-last jump and the crowd was going wild. But Owens regained the lead at 26-¾ and capped with competition with a final jump of 26-5 ½.

Long was second and, with the Fuhrer looking on, was the first person to congratulate Owens on his victory.

"You can melt down all the medals and cups I have, and they wouldn't be a plating on the 24-carat friendship I felt for Luz Long at that moment," Owens would later write.

Long would be killed in the Battle of St. Pietro on July 14, 1943. Owens would win two more gold medals in Berlin, in the 200 meters and the 400-meter relay, and hold the long jump world record for more than 25 years.

The next Olympics were scheduled for 1940 in Japan—Sapporo for the Winter Games, Tokyo for the Summer. But Japan and China went to war in 1938, and the Japanese cities withdrew. There then began an incredible period in which the IOC became the ostrich of the sports world and refused to believe what it was seeing.

Feeling it should stay out of world politics, the IOC moved the Winter Games to St. Moritz, Switzerland, and the Summer Games to Helsinki, Finland. That was not the end. The Swiss argued over IOC rules that classified ski instructors as professionals; so the IOC moved the Winter Games again, this time to Garmisch-Partenkirchen, Germany. That decision came in June 1939, after Germany had invaded Austria.

On September 1, 1939, Hitler's armies invaded Poland and two days later Britain and France declared war on Germany. Still, preparations continued for the Winter Games in Garmisch, and didn't stop until November 22. The following month, Finland was invaded by the Soviet Union, yet the IOC continued to plan for the Helsinki Games. It was not until the Finnish Olympic Committee formally withdrew as host in April 1940 that the IOC finally shelved plans for any Games that year.

In the midst of this shuffling, the IOC awarded the 1944 Games to Cortina d'Ampezzo, Italy (Winter) and London (Summer). With World War II still raging, these Games were called off, this time without any dance of denial.

All of these cities eventually would become Olympic hosts, but only after the passage of many years—and the loss of many, many lives.

Berlin Firsts

The 1936 Berlin Games are remembered most for the athletic feats of Jesse Owens against the background of Nazi propaganda and the approach of World War II. But they also contributed several milestones that have become key parts of the Olympics:

A list of Olympic firsts in Berlin includes:

TELEVISION. The medium was in its infancy and used the Berlin games as a laboratory. Huge cameras followed the action start to finish and telecast to the capital. There were few TV sets in those days, so 25 big-screen monitors were set up around the city for Berliners to watch the Games for free.

TORCH RELAY. Dr. Carl Diem, a member of the Berlin organizing committee and a close friend of Coubertin, devised a route from ancient Olympia, where the flame was lighted from rays of the sun, to the Reichsstadion. More than 3,000 athletes took part.

BASKETBALL. The first Olympic basketball tournament was staged outdoors on sandy clay tennis courts. The United States won its first of seven straight gold medals, beating Canada 19-8 in a heavy rainstorm.

OFFICIAL FILM. Hitler loved the propaganda value of movies and commissioned Leni Riefenstahl to capture the Berlin Games on film. The result was a classic documentary, *Olympische Spiele*, which portrays the Olympics in dark, haunting tones. Riefenstahl placed cameras low on the homestretch to record the end of distance races, set up a camera on a metal track to follow Owens through his sprints and even had photographers plunge off the 10-meter tower to record diving competition.

ABOVE: Bob Mathias, then a 17-year-old high school decathlon star, twirls the discus at the 1948 Games. He won the gold medal, his first of two.

BELOW: The 1948 decathlon gold medal comes closer for Bob Mathias, right, as he wins the 110-meter hurdles.

Olympics Face a New World

World War II would wipe out two Olympic years, 1940 and 1944, wasting the lives of many heroes of Games past and depriving thousands more of their peak com-

RIGHT: Fanny Blankers-Koen winning her heat of the 80-meter hurdles in a world record-equalling 11.3 seconds.

BELOW: She thought she was too old, but Fanny Blankers-Koen, No. 692, was a star at age 30, winning the women's 100 and 200 and 80-meter hurdles in 1948.

petitive years. The Olympic community essentially was placed on hold. By the time peace was restored in 1945 and the IOC began looking around for a site to stage the 1948 Games, it found a new world.

London, the choice to host the '44 Summer Games, was picked as the site for '48. Cortina d'Ampezzo was scrubbed as the Winter Games' site because of Italy's Axis role, and St. Moritz was picked in its place.

And despite the urging of president-elect Avery Brundage, the IOC refused to invite Germany or Japan to the post-war Olympic renewal.

The Winter Games were opened as a symbol of "a new world of peace and goodwill" by Swiss President Enrico Celio. Except for some warmer-than-expected weather, the St. Moritz Games went off without a hitch, and featured the Olympic debut of one of the great stars of the Winter Olympics, American figure skater Dick Button.

But staging the Winter Olympics in a neutral country such as Switzerland was one thing; holding the Summer Games in London, a city that took the pounding of the Blitz, was quite another. Some corners had to be cut.

Britain was still in the throes of wartime rationing, with food, gasoline and building materials in short supply. So organizers decided to eliminate an Olympic Village, housing the athletes instead in schools, military camps and private homes. Not a single new stadium or arena was built, but Britain was blessed with good facilities that had escaped the bombs and rockets of the Luftwaffe. Massive Wembley Stadium, perhaps the most hallowed soccer field on earth, was the main venue and the centerpiece of the Games.

Because of the 12-year gap and the major changes the war had wrought, London marked the debut of several athletes who were to become Olympic immortals.

Emil Zatopek of Czechoslovakia was an easy winner in the 10,000 meters, the first of his four Olympic gold medals. Boxer Laszlo Papp of Hungary won the first of three consecutive middleweight gold medals, and a 17-year-old from Tulare, California, Bob Mathias, won the decathlon gold, a medal he also would win in 1952.

But the biggest star of London was a Dutch mother of two, who at 30 was described even by her husband as "too old" to compete with the world's best.

Fanny Blankers-Koen had been an also-ran in Berlin as an 18-year-old, tying for sixth place in the high jump and running a leg on Holland's fifth-place 400-meter relay. She managed to stay in competition during the war and improved with each year, setting or helping to set world records in six individual events and three relays. And in London, she capped her Olympic career with one of the best performances ever by a female athlete at the Games.

Limited to three individual events, Blankers-Koen picked the 100- and 200-meter dashes and the 80-meter hurdles, and won them all. She then anchored the Dutch team to victory in the 400-meter relay.

All of this from someone who almost quit the Games midway through because she missed her children.

Blankers-Koen was back in 1952, when the Games took place in Helsinki. But a blood infection prevented her from repeating the feats of London. These Games belonged to Zatopek—and the big Red Bear.

Russia competed in the early Games and did little to distinguish itself. Its athletes won only one gold medal before the nation began a self-imposed Olympic exile that would last 40 years, spanning the overthrow of the czars and the creation of the Soviet Union.

Helsinki was the coming-out party for Soviet athletes and they immediately made their presence felt. Housed in a secluded camp on the outskirts of the Finnish capital—leaders

ABOVE: Emil Zatopek of Czechoslovakia strains to the finish of the 1948 10,000 meters. It was his first of four Olympic golds.

ABOVE: Weightlifter Jacob Kuzenko leads the first Olympic team from the Soviet Union into the stadium during opening ceremonies in Helsinki in 1952.

ABOVE RIGHT: Nina Romashkova, a discus thrower, won the first gold medal for the Soviet Union.

RIGHT: The United States team salutes as it passes the presidential box at the 1952 Helsinki Games.

in Moscow originally wanted to shuttle the athletes in by train or ferry just before their events—the Soviets welcomed their rivals with caviar and traded training techniques.

They also erected a big scoreboard to highlight the competition between themselves and the athletes from the United States. And there were plenty of victories to boast about.

Nina Romashkova, best known before the Olympics for being arrested in London on charges of shoplifting five hats, won the first gold medal for the Soviet Union in the women's discus by an amazing 14 feet, 3 inches over teammate Yelisaveta Bagryantseva. The world record-holder, Nina Dumbadze, completed the Soviet medal sweep with the bronze.

With strong showings in track, wrestling and gymnastics, the Soviet Union led the medal chart through the early stages of the Helsinki Games. But their scoreboard was wiped clean when American athletes—led by five gold medals from the boxing team—

passed them in the closing days. The United States wound up with more medals, 76-71, and more golds, 40-22. But the Soviets had shown that they were ready for worldwide competition at the highest levels and—with their client

58

ABOVE: This pole vault helped Bob Mathias win his second consecutive Olympic decathlon gold medal in 1952.

BELOW: American C.J. Capozzoli leads in the first turn of a heat of the 5,000 meters at Helsinki. Emil Zatopek won the gold.

ABOVE: Horace Ashenfelter, No. 998, trails the field early in the 1952 Olympic steeplechase. The America would rally to win the gold medal.

states of Eastern Europe—would dominate the Games for almost 40 years.

Zatopek was the dominating force on the track in Helsinki. A shoe factory worker who didn't start running until he was 18, Zatopek combined great stamina with bursts of speed that could catch and exhaust his rivals. He liked to run out front, and his awkward style—shoulders rolling, head bobbing about—made him look like a man struggling for his last breath. The grimace on his face belied the ease with which he handled his challengers. "I am not talented enough to run and smile at the same time," he would explain.

In Helsinki, Zatopek successfully defended the title in the 10,000 meters and added the 5,000, the first runner to accomplish the distance double since Hannes Kolehmainen of Finland in 1912.

With two gold medals in his pockets, Zatopek decided to try for one more. He never had run a marathon, but why not give it a go?

So on the final day of the Games, there was Zatopek, running at the head of the marathon field with Jim Peters of Britain, considered the best in the world. The early pace was blistering, and Zatopek carried on a conversation with Peters for several miles before the marathon rookie sped away from the faltering veteran, who dropped out with leg cramps after 20 miles. Zatopek kept going, pulling far ahead of the field as he chatted with fans along the route. He entered the stadium to cries of "Za-to-pek! Za-to-pek!" from the crowd of more than 70,000. After he crossed the finish line, Zatopek was picked up by members of the Jamaican 1,600-meter relay team, who carried

him around the track. He was signing autographs by the time silver-medalist Reinaldo Gorno completed the race, and Zatopek greeted him with an orange slice.

The marathon took so much out of Zatopek that he was unable to walk for a week. "But it was the most pleasant exhaustion I have ever known," he said.

For 1956, the Olympics traveled Down Under. Melbourne, Australia, was the place, the first time the Games had been held in the Southern Hemisphere, and they opened amid global tension that was to be felt throughout the competition.

The Soviet Union had invaded Hungary on November 4, less than three weeks before the Games began. In the Middle East, the Suez Canal crisis was brewing. These two events led to the first Olympic boycotts. The Netherlands, Spain and Switzerland withdrew to protest the Soviet invasion, while Egypt, Iraq and Lebanon pulled out over Suez. There were widespread calls for the Games to be canceled, but IOC President Avery Brundage—long an opponent of political interference in the Olympics—would not hear of it. "We will not let any country use the Olympics for political purposes," Brundage declared. It was a speech he would have to make over and over before his reign expired in 1972.

The Hungarian team already had started the long journey to Melbourne before the tanks rolled into Budapest. They chose to compete as scheduled. Greeted by refugees and other well-wishers at the airport upon their arrival, the athletes sang "God Bless Hungary" and tore down the Communist flag over their headquarters at the Olympic Village. When they marched in the opening ceremonies, some of the Hungarian team members did not have uniforms, having left them in the chaos back home. They received wave after wave of cheers from the crowd at the Melbourne Cricket Ground. At the end of the Games, half the Hungarian team refused to go back to Budapest.

The Soviet Union had a big team in Melbourne, and athletes from the two

ABOVE: Emil Zatopek duels with Alexandr Anoufriev of the Soviet Union in a heat of the 5,000 meters in Helsinki. Anoufriev won the heat but Zatopek took the gold medal.

LEFT: IOC President Avery Brundage addresses the closing ceremonies of the 1956 Games in Melbourne.

LEFT: Charlie Jenkins of the United States winning the 400 meters at Melbourne in 46.7 seconds.

BELOW: Bobby Morrow breaks the tape to win the 100-meter gold medal in Melbourne.

BELOW RIGHT: Lazlo Papp of Hungary, right, defeated American Jose Torres for his third straight light-middleweight gold medal in Melbourne.

BELOW LEFT: Al Oerter uncorks a discus throw in Melbourne. He won the gold medal, his first of an unprecedented four in a row.

LEFT: While the 1956 Olympics were held in Melbourne, Australian quarantine laws forced the equestrian events to be staged in Stockholm. The dressage medalists were, left to right, Lise Hartel of Denmark, silver; Henri de St. Cyr, Sweden, gold; and Liselott Linsenhoff, Germany, bronze.

BOTTOM: The Soviet invasion of Hungary just before the 1956 Games brought Cold War friction to Melbourne. Valentine Prokopov, a star of the Soviet water polo team, was involved in an in-the-water fight with Ervin Zader of Hungary.

countries competed more or less without conflict—with one notable exception.

Hungary had the world's best water polo team, and when it played the Soviet Union in the semifinals two days before the end of the Games, on December 6, all of its passion spilled out. There literally was blood in the pool. The contest turned into a brawl and the referee stopped it with Hungary leading 4-0. Police had been called in to protect the Soviet players from members of the crowd.

Australia is, in essence, a very big island and over the years has imposed strict quarantine laws to protect its livestock. Because of this, the Melbourne Games were the only Olympics to be held in two countries. Equestrian events were staged in Stockholm, Sweden, earlier in the year, with their own opening and closing ceremonies and Olympic flame.

Despite the water-polo battle between Hungary and the Soviet Union, the Melbourne Olympics were heralded as "the Friendly Games." One reason for that lasting image was the closing ceremonies, when athletes broke ranks and danced with each other in a spontaneous outpouring of friendship. It was the first time it happened, and it has become an Olympic tradition.

The tradition for 1960 was ancient Rome. The Coliseum and the Forum provided the backdrop for Games that were among the most exciting in history—and marked the end of an era.

The Rome Olympics featured big performances by big names. Wilma Rudolph, who

RIGHT: Ivan Tregubov of the Soviet Union tries to block a shot by Canada's Billy Colvin in the gold-medal hockey game in 1956. The Soviets won 2-0 to begin a domination of Olympic hockey that lasted almost four decades.

BELOW: Sixten Jernberg of Sweden wins the 50-kilometer cross-country race at the Winter Games in Cortina d'Ampezzo.

RIGHT: The Olympic flame leaves ancient Olympia in Greece on the start of a relay to Rome for the 1960 Games.

overcame childhood polio and scarlet fever, won the women's 100- and 200-meters and anchored the U.S. 400-meter relay team to victory. Rafer Johnson of the United States edged C.K. Yang, his close friend and UCLA teammate from Taiwan, for the decathlon gold medal. Another American, Ralph Boston, won the long jump and broke Jesse Owens' 24-year-old Olympic record at 26 feet, 7 ¾ inches. And the men's 100 featured one of the closest finishes ever, with Germany's Armin Hary edging Dave Sime of the United States for the gold. Both were timed in 10.2 seconds and all six sprinters were timed within .02 seconds of each other.

LEFT: Rafer Johnson won the decathlon in Rome in a stirring duel with Taiwan's C.K. Yang. The American took the shot put with a throw of 51 feet, 10 3-4 inches.

ABOVE: Peter Snell of New Zealand edged world record-holder Roger Moens (No. 237) for the 800-meter gold medal in Rome.

BELOW: The 100 meters in Rome was supposed to an American lock, but Armin Hary of Germany, extreme left, took the gold.

ABOVE: Wilma Rudolph swept the women's 100 and 200, and anchored the United States to victory in the 400-meter relay in Rome.

BELOW: Australia's Herb Elliott easily won the 1,500 meters in Rome in a world-record 3 minutes, 35.6 seconds. He finished 15 meters ahead of silver-medalist Michel Jazy of France.

Peter Snell of New Zealand won his first Olympic gold, in the 800 meters, and Herb Elliott of Australia ran away with the gold in the 1,500.

But the biggest star of the Games was a fast-talking kid from Kentucky. The world would get to know a lot more about him over the next 30 years.

"The Louisville Lip" was what they called 18-year-old Cassius Clay, and it seemed as if those lips were always moving. He won the light-heavyweight gold medal with a unanimous decision over Zbigniew Pietrzykowski of Poland, a three-time European champion and the veteran of 231 fights. The way he fought, however, was only part of Clay's appeal. He loved the Roman crowds and bantered with them incessantly. He spouted poetry and always had a quote for the press. He went out of his way to let people know he was an American and proud of it, despite growing racial tensions.

Clay, of course, went on to become the world heavyweight champion and take a much different view of life from the one he professed in Rome. He adopted Islam, changed his name to Muhammad Ali and became a social force in civil rights and anti-war movements. In his autobiography, "The

LEFT: Ralph Boston works out at the U.S. training camp near Rome. Boston won the long jump with a leap of 26 feet, 7 3-4 inches, breaking Jesse Owens' 24-year-old Olympic record.

BELOW: Members of the team from Taiwan entered the Rome Olympic stadium protesting the IOC's order that their country be identified as Formosa instead of the Republic of China.

ABOVE: A young American boxer named Cassius Clay scored a unanimous decision over Poland's Zbigniew Pietrzykowski for the light-heavyweight gold medal in Rome. Clay converted to Islam, changed his name to Muhammad Ali, and became perhaps the world's best-known athlete.

Greatest," Ali tells what happened to his Olympic gold medal: He threw it into the Ohio River after a fight with members of a white motorcycle gang, which started after the boxer and a friend were refused service in a Louisville restaurant because they were black. "The medal was gone," he wrote, "but I felt calmly relaxed, confident. My holiday as a White Hope was over. I felt new, secret strength."

That strength and his willingness to endure criticism and persecution, while retaining a true love and understanding of all people, helped Ali to become the most famous athlete—and perhaps the most famous person—in the world.

As the world changed Ali, so it was about to change the Olympics. In many ways, Rome was the last of the Games staged like a county fair. From then on, it would turn into a worldwide five-ring circus.

The Barefoot Champion

On the Appian Way, about a mile from the Arch of Constantine, stands an obelisk. It's old, but among the glories of Rome it's not a major tourist attraction. Just a big pillar. But there's a story to the obelisk. It was stolen by Roman troops from Axum, an ancient kingdom that would become what we know as Ethiopia. And that made it the perfect spot for Abebe Bikila to make his move in the Olympic marathon.

Bikila was a 28-year-old private in the Imperial Bodyguards who protected Ethiopian Emperor Haile Selassie. He had run two marathons in his life before the Olympics, and was considered a rank outsider.

Ah, but Bikila had a plan. He knew that distance running in his hometown of Mout, about 8,100 feet above sea level, had conditioned his lungs and legs for endurance. And he believed that—if he kept near the front of

the pack—he could outrace anyone in the late stages of the contest.

The marathon was to be run at night, along the ancient cobblestones of the "Queen of Roads." Several days before the race, Bikila and his coach, Onni Niskanen of Sweden, surveyed the course and came upon the obelisk of Axum, at the bottom of a slight incline one mile from the finish line at the arch. It's just the place, they agreed, to make that final charge and "make some history for Africa."

When the race started, about the only thing that distinguished Bikila from the rest of the field were his shoes—he wasn't wearing any. The barefoot bodyguard bided his time in the pack, sneaking toward the front through the early miles and finally edging to the front about midway through. With Bikila was Rhadi Ben Abdesselem of Morocco, a highly touted runner, and together they clipped off 5-minute miles one after the other.

At the 22-mile mark they were stride for stride. It looked as if Abdesselem had Bikila right where he wanted him.

And then they reached the obelisk of Axum.

Bikila just blew Abdesselem away. He charged up the hill and never looked back, building a 200-yard lead over the final mile. Bikila's biggest problem was avoiding a motor scooter, which had mistakenly been driven onto the course 60 yards from the end.

The winning time was 2 hours, 15 minutes, 16.2 seconds, a world best. It earned Bikila a promotion to sergeant and a new Volkswagen.

Four years later, wearing shoes this time, Bikila won the Olympic marathon again—less than six weeks after having his appendix removed. This time, Bikila was made a lieutenant in the bodyguards. But that old VW he received for his first gold medal was to take him on a tragic path. In 1969, Bikila was driving the car when it collided with another vehicle. He was paralyzed from the waist down and confined to a wheelchair until his death from a brain hemorrhage in 1973.

CHAPTER IX

Olympics Turn to the East

When an Air Force rocket launched a tiny little satellite named Telstar in the early 1960s, the whole world shrank. That downsizing would help the Olympics expand beyond expectations and finally accomplish the goal of true internationalism, the root of Coubertin's revival of the Games almost 70 years before.

LEFT: More than 80,000 people jammed Tokyo's Olympic Stadium for the opening ceremonies of the 1964 Games.

ABOVE: Joe Frazier beat Germany's Hans Huber for the 1964 heavyweight gold medal.

ABOVE RIGHT: Don Schollander anchored the U.S. men's 400-meter freestyle relay team to a gold in a world-record 3 minutes, 33.2 seconds in Tokyo.

The Tokyo Games in 1964 were the first beneficiary of this new satellite network of global communication. In Rome, videotape, a new form of transcribing visual images, was used to provide viewers with same-day coverage of events. The tape still had to be flown from Rome to New York for American networks to use it, but it didn't have to be compactness of the video cameras used helped the fan get close to the action and the athletes. It helped make Cassius Clay a star, and the American boxer would learn the lessons of direct communication through television very well.

With Telstar and similar satellites, the Games moved right into the living rooms of the world. Signals from the Olympics could be bounced off the satellites and picked up by antennas at network headquarters, where they were broadcast live over traditional television channels. A race that was run in Japan was seen split-seconds later in New Jersey. Satellite time was expensive, and the difference in time zones—a 14-hour head start on the U.S. East Coast—made timing for maximum audiences tough. But the start had been made, and the television connection would prove to be the savior—if also the occasional curse—of the Olympic community.

The cameras in Tokyo caught some of the most dramatic and poignant Olympic moments ever. These Games were to have been held in 1940, but the Sino-Japanese War forced Tokyo to withdraw. Then came World War II and Japan, like Germany, was barred from the first post-war renewal, in 1948. Some thought the old capital never would host the Games, but the IOC finally relented in 1959 and awarded the '64 Games to the world's largest city.

Tokyo went all out. It spent some $3 billion on new stadiums, arenas and infrastructure. These were the first computerized games, with scoring and timekeeping all done electronically. The Tokyo computer was huge and fully state of the art for 1964; today, we can find the same memory capacity in a handheld calculator.

The architecture for the Games was internationally praised, a subtle mix of ancient Shinto shapes with modern building techniques that gave the massive buildings a sense of calm and intimacy.

Throughout the Games, however, athletes found ways to shatter that calm.

Don Schollander of the United States became the first swimmer to win four gold medals in a single Games when he won the 100- and 200-meter freestyle and anchored two winning freestyle relay teams. Dawn Fraser of Australia won the women's 100 freestyle for a record third consecutive Olympics, a triumph tinged with tragedy. Just seven months earlier, Fraser had suffered a broken neck in a car crash that killed her mother. The swimmer was in a neck brace for more than six weeks after the accident but trained hard once the cast came off and won in an Olympic-record 59.5 seconds.

Fraser's Olympic career ended on a less happy note. She was arrested for stealing a flag from the emperor's palace in a midnight raid by a group of athletes. Although charges were dropped and the emperor gave her the flag as a gift, Fraser was suspended for 10 years by the Australian Swimming Union.

Another Frazier was the hit of the boxing tournament. Joe Frazier was a real-life Rocky, working in a Philadelphia meat locker by day and training by night for the Olympics. He lost to Buster Mathis in the U.S. trials and went to Tokyo as a sparring partner. But Mathis broke a finger in training and Frazier stepped in. He moved through the field, and reached the semifinals, where he beat Vadim Yemelyanov of the Soviet Union. Frazier came out of that bout with a broken left thumb, but refused to be X-rayed. "I got to get this gold medal," he said. "It's the only way I can get out of the slaughterhouse." The next day he decisioned Hans Huber of Germany for the gold medal. He would go on to become heavyweight champion of the world.

In track, Bob Hayes proved he was the world's fastest human. he ran away with the

ABOVE: Billy Mills, raised in a family of 15 childen on a Sioux reservation in South Dakota, surprised the world by winning the 10,000-meter gold medal in Tokyo with a sprint through the stretch.

gold medal in the 100 meters, winning by 7 feet over Enrique Figuerola of Cuba and equalling the world record of 10 seconds flat. Wyomia Tyus of the United States won the women's 100, her first of two straight, and Peter Snell of New Zealand added to the 800-meter gold he won in Rome by taking the 800 and the 1,500, the first man to accomplish that feat since 1920.

Hayes, Tyus and Snell all were favorites who came through. The same could not be said of Billy Mills. Come through he did, but as a decided outsider.

Mills was one of 15 children, born and raised on the Oglala Sioux reservation in South Dakota. He was an orphan by the

ABOVE: Billy Mills brushes off an attempt to pass by Mohammad Gammoudi of Tunisia in the 10,000 at Tokyo. Mills won in 28 minutes, 24.4 seconds -- 46 seconds faster than his previous personal best.

time he was 12 and moved to an Indian boarding school in Kansas. Running was part of his training for boxing at first but it eventually became his sport and won him a scholarship to the University of Kansas.

Mills was a specialist in the longest track race, the 10,000 meters. He was steady, never spectacular, and in 1962—while a lieutenant in the Marines—he quit running.

If not for his wife's urging, Mills might never have achieved the defining moment of his life.

Pat Mills was a track nut and wanted her husband to get back to the sport. She dragged him to meets as a spectator, hoping it would revive his interest. It did. Mills

resumed running and made the U.S. team for Tokyo in both the 10,000 and the marathon.

In the 10,000 meters, Mills was entered among one of the greatest fields in history, headed by defending champion Pyotr Bolotnikov of the Soviet Union and world record-holder Ron Clarke of Australia. Personal bests for many in the field were a full minute faster than Mills', an immense amount of time to overcome even in a race so long.

Mills was undaunted. His plan was to stay in the middle of he pack and accelerate on every other lap, picking off runners gradually as he inched his way to front. Halfway through the race he was fifth, with Clarke in the lead, but Mills was worried about the fast pace of 14 minutes, 6 seconds at the 5,000 mark and even considered dropping out.

"At one point I was going to go one more lap, take the lead and go one more," he said. "That way if I did quit it would be while I was winning. I was thinking that if I had to quit, I wasn't going to do it in front of where Pat was sitting; I'd do it at the other end of the field."

There was no quit in Mills this day, though. He stalked Clarke lap after lap, sometimes dropping as much as 15 yards behind and then charging forward. With 1,000 meters remaining, the race was down to Clarke, Mills and Mohammad Gammoudi of Tunisia. The race was moving at a 29-minute pace, much faster than Mills or Gammoudi ever had run, and Clarke seemed to have a lock on the gold medal. But then Clarke glanced over his shoulder and Mills knew he still had a chance.

"I saw him look back, and I thought, 'My gosh, he's worried.'" Mills recalled. "From that point on I stayed with him."

With the track littered with slower runners being lapped, Clarke, Mills and Gammoudi entered the final 400 meters dodging from left to right. At the top of the backstretch, Mills boxed in Clarke behind a slower runner and Clarke had to push his way out of trouble. It started a real shoving match, and at one point Mills thought he was going to fall. His legs started to buckle. Then Gammoudi pushed through and took the lead, and the final sprint was on after almost six miles. Mills appeared to be out of it, some 15 yards off the lead as they rounded the final turn, but the cheering of the crowd of 75,000 kept him going.

Clarke and Gammoudi exchanged the lead as they entered the stretch. With 80 yards to go, Mills felt good. "We came off the last curve and I could see the tape stretched across the finish line," he said. "Then I thought, 'I can win, I can win.'"

Mills' sprint through the stretch caught Clarke and then Gammoudi. He felt the tape break across his chest. He was the Olympic champion, in an Olympic record 28 minutes, 24.4 seconds—46 seconds faster than he had ever run the 10,000 before.

For the home fans, there were two moments in Tokyo that stood out—one of great joy, one of terrible despair.

The Japanese women's volleyball team became national heroes as they went undefeated to win the gold medal. The championship match against the Soviet Union was watched by some 80 percent of Japanese television viewers. The tournament was played without the best team in the world, from North Korea, which was banned by the IOC for participating in unsanctioned events in Indonesia the previous year.

But the elation Japan felt over its volleyball gold was balanced by near humiliation in the national sport of judo. The Japanese ex-

BELOW: The United States swept the 100-meter gold medals in Tokyo, with Wyomia Tyus, shown here, winning the women's sprint and Bob Hayes the men's.

pected their judo fighters to clean up in the events, held in the Olympics for the first time, and waited for the sweep to be completed by Akio Kaminaga, the national champion in the unlimited class. But Kaminaga was upset by Anton Geesink, a 267-pound Dutchman. When Geesink won 9 minutes, 22 seconds into the match, the judo hall fell silent. Eventually, polite applause greeted the victory of Geesink, who is now an IOC member.

The Tokyo Games were filled with joy, from the dancers at the opening ceremonies to "Sayonara" flashed in giant computer letters on the scoreboard closing night. Japan had hosted a near-perfect Games, and used the success as a signal that it had made it back from the ravages of war and re-entered the world as a full, respected member. It was a strategy to be used again and again by Olympic hosts as the Games grew bigger—and the pricetag and other burdens of hosting grew right along.

ABOVE: An actress dressed as the high priestess of Ancient Olympia holds aloft the flame for the 1968 Summer Games in Mexico City.

BELOW: Protesters scramble around a police bus in Mexico City after a night of riots and army gunfire in which 260 people were killed. The demonstrations opposed government spending on Olympic projects.

The Games in Turmoil

B lack power. Vietnam. Urban riots. Protest marches. Getting drafted. Getting stoned.

So much happened in the wake of the happy, jolly Games of Tokyo. The world was shrinking, that was true. People were being exposed to cultures and beliefs they never knew existed. And as distances became smaller, they brought along new problems. It was the same for the Olympics as for the rest of the world.

The Olympics declare themselves a festival of the world's youth, and in the late 1960s that youth was very restless. The television generation had seen the assassinations of a president, his brother and a beloved civil rights leader. It was fighting an increasingly unpopular war in Southeast Asia, and bringing that war to the streets and college campuses in protests that sometimes turned violent. At a time when all seemed to be questioning something about their culture and themselves, athletes for the first time started looking at what they did and how their performances were viewed by others. Many did not like the portrait that appeared.

It was in this environment of anti-establishment feeling and quest for something new that the Olympics moved to Latin America—to Mexico City, the mile-high capital of a country that loved sports but also was ensnared in social and political problems on a mammoth scale.

Mexico's economy was crumbling. Poverty was at epidemic proportions, and many people saw the hundreds of millions of dollars being spent on Olympic facilities as a true waste of money. Mexican students staged protest demonstrations against spending for the Games, but the IOC and Mexican authorities would not be moved. The confrontation climaxed just 10 days before the opening ceremonies.

On the night of October 2, 1968, 10,000 demonstrators marched into downtown Mexico City, in the Square of the Three Cultures, protesting government policies.

BELOW: Tommie Smith celebrates as he wins the 200 meters in Mexico City, with teammate John Carlos third. Note the black sox Smith and Carlos wore as a civil-rights protest.

They were met by the Mexican army. Gunfire erupted and 260 people were killed. Another 1,200 were wounded.

There were calls for the Games to be delayed or called off. As always, IOC President Avery Brundage said he never would bow to political pressure and the Olympics opened on schedule, with troops and tanks everywhere and a cloud of tension clinging to the stadiums.

The tension was not just from outside sources. The athletes wanted to be heard, as well.

Black power was at its height in the inner cities and poor rural areas of the United States. A sizeable portion of the U.S. team came from those ghettoes, and they brought along black berets and power salutes along with their spikes and sweatsuits.

Their protests began before the Games, when the IOC voted to rescind its eight-year-old ban on South Africa over apartheid. The American blacks joined with athletes from Africa and the Soviet Union in threatening to withdraw if South Africa was allowed back in. With Mexican organizers fearful that such a boycott would ruin the Games, the IOC backed down and kept South Africa out.

The Games opened on schedule on October 12, with a woman, 400-meter runner Enriqueta Basilio, lighting the Olympic flame for the first time. But unlike the thousands of brightly colored balloons released at the opening ceremonies, the protests and social statements did not blow away.

Two of the best athletes at the Games used their success as a stage to vent their anger.

Tommie Smith and John Carlos were among the fastest sprinters in the world. Teammates at San Jose State, they also were members of a group called the Olympic Project for Human Rights, run by a San Jose State professor, Harry Edwards, which protested the treatment of American blacks. In the 200, both qualified for the final in 20.1 seconds, and in the race for the gold Smith—despite a pulled groin

muscle that almost scratched him from the race—won with a burst of speed in a world-record 19.83 seconds. Carlos, the previous world record-holder, was third in 20.10, giving up the silver medal when he glanced at a celebrating Smith in the final strides and allowed Peter Norman, a member of the Salvation Army from Australia, to sneak in second. The race was spectacular, but the real sensation was still to come.

On the medals stand, Carlos and Smith wore black socks and no shoes, civil rights buttons on their uniform jackets and black gloves on one hand. When "The Star-Spangled Banner" was played, the gold and bronze medalists bowed their heads and raised their gloved fists in the air, in the Black Power salute. "White America

ABOVE: Black Power salutes during the national anthem by 200-meter gold-medalist Tommie Smith and bronze medalist John Carlos got them kicked off the U.S. Olympic team.

RIGHT: Bill Toomey stands at attention during "The Star-Spangled Banner" after receiving the decathlon gold medal in Mexico City.

will only give us credit for an Olympic victory," Carlos said later. "They'll say I'm an American, but if I did something bad, they'd say I was a Negro."

At their news conference, Smith and Carlos said they bowed their heads because the words of freedom in the national anthem applied only to whites, not blacks. Their salute, they said, symbolized black strength and unity, their bare feet black poverty.

The IOC did not accept their explanations. It told the U.S. Olympic Committee that Smith and Carlos must be punished, and the USOC quickly threw them off the team and ordered them out of the Olympic Village.

At a time of such heightened tensions and polarized feelings on race, the actions of Smith and Carlos were loudly condemned by the rest of the Olympic establishment and by commentators throughout America. But the protests did not stop when they left the Games.

Lee Evans considered pulling out of the 400 in defiance of Smith and Carlos' expulsion. He ran instead, setting a world record, and then appeared to claim his gold medal in the same black-stockinged outfit his ousted teammates had worn, adding a black beret. Larry James and Ron Freeman, the silver and bronze medalists who also were black, joined him in the protest. When these three teamed with Vince Matthews to win the 1,600-meter relay, all four wore black berets on the podium and gave the Black Power salute. They were not disciplined.

The Black Power demonstrations overshadowed what was probably the greatest track meet in history. Critics had feared that Mexico City's altitude of 7,100 feet would produce problems for athletes and performances tainted by the thin air. They were right in both cases.

One of the first races was the 10,000 meters, and it didn't take long for the rare atmosphere to take effect. World record-holder Ron Clarke lasted until late in the slowly-run race and then dropped out with fatigue and blurred vision. The distance events were dominated by athletes from the highlands of Africa, such as 10,000-meter champion Naftali Temu of Kenya.

Overall, 10 world records and 16 Olympic records were set in track and field in Mexico City, with a world or Olympic mark established in every race from 1,500 meters on down. The ultimate mark—and the ultimate salute to the wonders of competing at altitude—was set in the long jump.

Bob Beamon put the world record so far out there, at 29 feet, 2 ½ inches, that any feat far beyond the norm has come to be called "Beamonesque." Even the jumper couldn't believe it when it happened.

"Mine was a jump way before its time," Beamon once said.

It came on a dark, cloudy afternoon, against a field that included the defending Olympic champion, Lynn Davies of Britain; and the co-holders of the world record, Ralph Boston of the United State and Igor Ter-Ovanesyan of the Soviet Union. Their mark: 27-4 ¾.

But Beamon was the favorite. He had won 22 of 23 meets coming into the Olympics, despite being suspended from the track team at Texas-El Paso because he refused to compete against Brigham Young University. In keeping with the times, Beamon had argued that BYU, affiliated with the Mormon church, was racist.

A 6-foot-3, 157-pounder from New York City, Beamon had a habit of fouling in prelims, and he followed the pattern in Mexico City. He fouled his first two jumps but qualified on his final attempt, after getting some advice from Boston to adjust his stride.

That's as close as the rest of the jumpers would get to beating Beamon, and as close as he would come to being mortal at the Olympics.

Beamon was the fourth jumper in the finals. The first three fouled, and Boston encouraged him to "make this a good one" as he approached the runway. Beamon's secret was speed on the approach—he was timed in 9.5 seconds for the 100-yard dash—and he nailed his takeoff right at the end of the board.

Pictures from that day show Beamon high in the air, his knees up, his arms stretched in front of him, his mouth gasping for air and his eyes—his eyes looked as if he had just gone to the edge of the earth and peered over.

He hung in the air for an incredibly long time and landed solidly in the pit. He had gone into another world.

Boston told Davies he thought Beamon was beyond 28 feet. The electronic measuring device at the long jump pit could not tell—Beamon had landed beyond its range. Officials finally pulled out an old-fashioned tape measure and started their calculations. They checked and rechecked, and finally posted the distance in meters—8.90, compared with Boston and Ter-Ovanesyan's old mark of 8.35.

"Compared to this jump," Ter-Ovanesyan told Davies, "the rest of us are as children."

Beamon knew he had the world record, but—as most Americans—had trouble converting metric distances to feet and inches. He stood around while officials converted it for him. And when it was announced at 29-2 ½, Beamon was beyond belief. His legs gave out, and he sank to his knees, resting his forehead on the track. He remained there for several minutes, delaying the start of the men's 400. Doctors later said

BELOW: Bob Beamon in his record-breaking long-jump at the 1968 Olympics in Mexico.

Beamon had suffered a cataleptic seizure, shocked into numbness by the magnitude of his own accomplishment.

The rest of this great field was humbled. No one else broke 27 feet, with Klaus Beer of Germany winning the silver at 26-10 ½.

Everybody jumped at the same altitude. Everyone had the same stiff-but-legal breeze of 2 meters per second at their backs. But no one came within 2 ½ feet of Beamon that day.

No one approached his mark for more than two decades. Mike Powell of the United States finally jumped longer—29-4 ½, at the 1991 World Championships in Tokyo.

Millions of people worldwide saw Beamon's record-shattering performance live. The television revolution that had started in Tokyo was now in high gear. It was paying the IOC more money—just under $10 million in worldwide rights fees in 1964—and making the Games the most-watched sports event in the world. But that exposure also made the Olympics the world's biggest stage, as the protests of Smith, Carlos and the others had shown. And that stage would soon be covered in blood.

Munich in 1972 was supposed to wipe away so much. West Germany desperately

ABOVE: Bob Beamon is overcome by emotion after breaking the long-jump record.

RIGHT: Debbie Meyer of the United States winning the 800-meter freestyle, her third gold medal of the Mexico City Games.

ABOVE: .Bill Toomey in the long-
jump portion of the decathlon.
He won the event on his way to
the gold medal.

BELOW: A true ironman of sports,
Al Oerter won his fourth
consecutive discus gold medal
in Mexico City, an
unprecedented streak.

wanted to stage a friendly, open Olympics. It wanted to finally close the book on its ostracism following World War II and highlight its subsequent development into one of the most dynamic economies in the world. And it wanted to erase the memories of Hitler's Nazi propaganda and racism in Berlin 36 years before.

Everything the Munich organizing committee did in the buildup to the Games worked as they hoped. The main stadium,

swimming hall and basketball arena were built on parkland just outside the city. Their plastic and glass roofs, suspended from giant poles, were invitingly futuristic. In contrast to the cold, enclosed, squared-off look of Berlin, everything in Munich seemed wide open, free and easy.

Why, even the Olympic Village would be open. There would be security checks, of course, but—hey, we're all friends here.

The task fell to Willi Daume, a member of the German Olympic basketball team in 1936. He was a successful businessman and one of the friendliest people you would care to meet. He set up an organization both efficient and open to suggestion. Things were done on time, on budget and aimed at satisfying the athletes and fans.

Who could ask for more? More than $3 billion was spent, including the construction of a new subway line to get fans to and from the venues. The world was coming to Munich—7,800 athletes from a record 122 countries—and it would get a hearty Bavarian welcome.

ABOVE: Californian Mark Spitz wins the swimming gold at the Munich Games.

RIGHT: Mark Spitz in the 200-meter butterfly finals in 1972.

When the Games started August 26, all seemed perfect. And the athletes did their best to show off the spectacular setting.

Mark Spitz was the biggest hero, winning a record seven gold medals with seven world record in swimming. Lasse Viren of Finland won the 5,000 and 10,000 meters. Olga Korbut, dubbed the "Munich Munchkin," won a gold medal in the women's floor exercises with a combination of athletic excellence and teen-age exuberance and sparked a worldwide interest in gymnastics. In the marathon, Frank Shorter of the United States recorded a surprising victory and helped to start the running boom.

Munich also witnessed some of the most bizarre officiating and actions by organizers in Olympic history.

At the top of the list, of course, was the gold-medal basketball game between the United States and the Soviet Union. Rules interpretations that could be described as curious at best gave the Soviets three chances at the winning field goal. Sasha Belov finally put the ball in as time expired to give the Soviets a 50-49 victory that ended the U.S. unbeaten streak in the Olympics at 62 games. The United States appealed the outcome but it was rejected 3-2—all East bloc members of a special review panel voting to uphold the victory,

both Western members voting to disallow Belov's bucket. In protest, the U.S. team failed to appear for the awards ceremonies and never accepted their silver medals, which remain in an IOC vault in Lausanne.

Another U.S. athlete lost a gold medal to drugs—not steroids, but asthma medicine.

Rick Demont won the 400-meter freestyle but tested positive for ephedrine, a banned stimulant contained in his prescription asthma spray. Demont had told officials at the start of the meet that he had been using the medicine for two years. The officials never told him it was illegal.

Two other groups of athletes who did come up with medals were expelled from the Games.

ABOVE: Kathy Rigby on the balance beam in Munich. The young American was a great gymnast but no match at the Olympics for Eastern European stars such as Olga Korbut.

LEFT: Frank Shorter grabs a drink near the halfway mark of the Munich Olympic marathon on his way to the gold medal.

First, the Pakistan hockey team was angered when West Germany beat it in the gold-medal game, storming the judges' table and pouring water over the heads of officials. When the medals were handed out, the Pakistanis refused to face the flag as the West German anthem was played. The IOC banned the Pakistani players for life, but reinstated them for the next Games in 1976.

Then, in a scene reminiscent of Mexico City, American 400-meter runners Vince Matthews and Wayne Collett were handed lifetime Olympic bans after collecting their gold and silver medals. The IOC was angered when Matthews, who had taken part in the Black Power protests four years earlier, and Collett talked to each other and failed to stand at attention while "The Star-Spangled Banner" was played.

Other music filled the Munich Games. It was a funeral dirge, and all people paid attention.

Early in the morning of September 5, the peace in that friendly, open Olympic Village was blown apart. Eight members of a Palestinian terrorist organization known

as Black September invaded the village and broke into apartments on Connollystrasse housing the Israeli team. Armed with machine guns, the terrorists killed two Israelis immediately and rounded up nine others as hostages. Their demands: Release some 200 Palestinians held on terrorist charges in Israel, and allow themselves to flee to safety.

Almost immediately, the open spaces of the village became an armed camp. Television beamed live pictures around the world of one terrorist leader discussing the demands with a group including West German Interior Minister Hans-Dietrich Genscher. Another, haunting scene showed one of the terrorists, a black ski mask over his face and a machine gun on his back, keeping watch on the balcony of a village apartment.

Deadlines came and were extended. The sun came up and events were scheduled. Some of the morning competition took place. But by afternoon, no one's stomach was in the Games, and the rest of the day's competition was called off.

As night fell, officials agreed to allow the terrorists to take their hostages to a

TOP: Vince Matthews joyfully crosses the finish line to win the 400 meters in Munich ahead of U.S. teammate Wayne Collett.

BOTTOM LEFT: Terror in the Olympic Village. A Palestinian commando waits on the balcony of village apartment where Israeli athletes and coaches were taken hostage.

ABOVE: Matthews, right, and Collett both stood at-ease on the gold-medal stand as "The Star-Spangled Banner" was played. The athletes were booed by the crowd.

ABOVE: The coffin of Israeli weightlifter David Berger is loaded aboard a military cargo plane near Munich. Berger was among 11 Israeli athletes killed in the terrorist attack.

RIGHT: Protesters in Tel Aviv call for the Olympics to be stopped, following the slaying of 11 Israeli athletes and coaches.

military airfield by helicopter, then to be flown out of Germany. Sharpshooters were poised in the darkness. A first group left one of the helicopters. Shots were fired. A hand grenade exploded, blowing apart the second helicopter and its occupants.

All nine hostages were dead. So was a German policeman and five of the terrorists. The other three terrorists were captured.

It was the greatest tragedy ever to befall the Olympics. Although it had nothing to do with Munich or the Games, it happened there because of the intense, widespread attention the Olympics attract, at a time when terrorism in the Middle East was at its most violent.

Daume, his dream shattered, said it would be difficult to resume the Games. Teams from Norway and the Netherlands withdrew. But the IOC, in the form of Brundage, stood firm. This was to be Brundage's last Olympics as IOC president, and even a massacre would not sway his view that sport was one thing, politics—even when it involved terrorism—another.

The Olympics would mourn its fallen heroes with a one-day break. A memorial service was held at the Olympic Stadium, where the orchestra from the Munich Opera House played Beethoven's *Egmont Overture.* Daume spoke, and then Schmeul Lalkin, the Israeli team manager. He thanked the IOC for the respect shown by taking a break in the Games, and the German security forces for all they had done to try to save his athletes.

Finally, Brundage spoke, and his address made some wonder just what planet he was on.

He mourned the loss of the slain athletes and coaches. But he coupled this murderous invasion with another, nonviolent issue—the threat by black African nations to boycott the Games if white-ruled Rhodesia had been allowed to compete. The Olympics, Brundage said, had been "subjected to two savage attacks."

The next day, the Games resumed and ran out their final six days. They would never be the same.

The massacre at Munich left the Olympics shattered.

"These will be the last Olympic Games," Avery Brundage told his successor as IOC president, Lord Killanin, as he turned over the reigns of power at the end of the 1972 competition.

There wasn't much good to be said for the IOC or the Olympic community as a whole.

The Games had become a target for every political malcontent, and an easy target at that, if the events of 1968 in Mexico City and 1972 in Munich were any gauge.

What's more, they were almost broke. Despite the start of the television age a decade earlier and the large sums of money poured into the Olympics by local organizing committees, the IOC—the seat of power in Coubertin's grand design—was down to about $100,000, hardly enough to run its operation in Lausanne, Switzerland, for a few months.

And even four years ahead of time, the IOC knew it was facing more trouble in 1976.

Montreal, the beautiful city on the St. Lawrence River, had won the rights to host the '76 Games well before Munich. They were boom times for the world's economy, and Canada in general—the French-speaking province of Quebec in particular—was giddy with conspicuous wealth. So when organizers unveiled their models for Canada's first Olympics, centered on an island in the St. Lawrence, what people saw was something spectacular.

Huge stadiums and arenas with soaring roofs dotted the landscape. They seemed to rise from the ground and shoot upward. Because Montreal has long, cold winters and the city wanted to make sure its people got the most use out of the facilities once the Games left, just about everything—from swimming pools to cycling tracks—would be indoors. Even the main Olympic Stadium would have a roof—a retractable tent, anchored to a soaring tower that would hang over the stadium and provide those brave enough to ride an elevator 550 feet up the incline with a spectacular view of the city and the river valley.

Magnificent. But very, very expensive.

In the end, it was just too expensive. A combination of poor planning, grandiose budgeting, labor problems, short construction periods because of the cold weather and finally a general collapse of the economy in the wake of Middle Eastern oil boycotts left Montreal with egg on its face and big bills to pay.

The velodrome, budgeted at $19.7 million, wound up costing $86.5 million. The underground parking garages were sup-

ABOVE: Part of the multibillion-dollar construction projects Montreal undertook for the 1976 Games. In the foreground is the Olympic Village; in the background are the main stadium (right) and swimming hall.

posed to cost $20 million. Final price: $105 million.

And the Olympic Stadium topped all the overruns. The organizing committee said it would cost $132.5 million. By the time the Olympics began, the cost was $795.4 million—more than $100 million more than Munich had spent on *all* Olympic operations—and the stadium wasn't even finished. Not 80 cranes or 2,000 workers could complete the 60,000-seat structure and its cabled roof. The Games were opened and closed in a stadium that was a magnificent piece of architecture but one that also paid silent witness to the extravagances of the planning. At one end of the oval, where the tower for the roof had just begun to creep over the rim, sat a big construction crane. It would stay there long after the Olympics departed and become the symbol of the Montreal Games.

Montreal officials, who originally promised that the Games "wouldn't cost a penny," tried their best to see the good in all this.

"The future will be the judge," said Mayor Claude Drapeau, who was vilified for the overruns and poor image. "Anytime a man tries to do something that lasts beyond his own time, he has troubles. I doubt that anyone understood the significance of the Eiffel Tower, the Pyramids or the Sphinx."

Maybe not. But Paris of the turn of the century and the pharaohs of ancient Egypt never faced the kind of debt Montreal rolled up chasing its Olympic dream—more than $1 billion. It was enough to shake the government—and the IOC—and scare off potential Olympic bidders for years to come. The budget for just the Games was a record $1.2 billion, and included $100 million for a 16,000-member security force, a legacy of Munich's tragedy.

But money wasn't the only plague on Montreal's house. World politics created problems, too, including the first widespread boycott.

African nations were upset that the IOC allowed New Zealand to enter the Games, arguing that a tour of South Africa by the Pacific nation's rugby team violated the Olympic's anti-apartheid policy. Rugby wasn't an Olympic sport, but the protesters were solid in their determination. Led by Jean-Claude Ganga, a firebrand from the Congo, they beseeched the IOC to throw New Zealand out. Several accounts have documented how frustrated Ganga and his colleagues became when they were unable to take their case directly to Killanin. The way was blocked, these accounts say, by Monique Berlioux, the strong-willed director of the IOC who ran the committee day to day and was its de facto leader. Others privy to discussions aimed at preventing the boycott said the last straw was when IOC cars that were supposed to carry the African delegates to a meeting failed to show up. That's when Ganga pulled the plug, these sources say, and 24 African and Caribbean nations walked out of the Olympic village 48 hours before the opening ceremonies.

That was not all. The China issue was red hot, the heat turned up this time by the Canadian government.

Canada was among the first nations in the world to establish full relations with Beijing following President Richard Nixon's trip to the mainland in 1972. China was an important market for Canadian wheat and the government of Prime Minister Pierre Trudeau did not want to do anything to anger this vital customer. So it barred the team from Taiwan, the tiny island nation then known as the Republic of China, from entering Canada, arguing that the two nations had cut off diplomatic relations when Canada recognized Beijing. Mainland China was not recognized by the IOC, and would not send a team to the Olympics until 1984.

It was with some sense of relief, then, that the Games finally opened on July 17, 1976, with Britain's Queen Elizabeth delivering the welcome address.

And for the all the problems in the setup—and all the problems that would be left over—the Montreal Games were smashing.

They featured athletes who would become part of Olympic lore:

Nadia Comaneci, a 14-year-old Romanian gymnast, recorded the first perfect "10" on the bars and won two gold medals.

Bruce Jenner of the United States took the title of "world's greatest athlete" by winning the decathlon. Jenner was an all-American boy, with good looks, stylishly long hair and an ability to communicate. When he wrapped up the gold medal with a world-record total of 8,617 points, he waved a small American flag in triumph.

Alberto Juantorena of Cuba turned an unprecedented Olympic double in track, winning the 400 and 800 meters. Perhaps the greatest middle-distance runner of all time,

ABOVE: Nadia Comaneci became the first gymnast to register a perfect 10 when she won the uneven bars in Montreal. She later won the balance beam and all-around golds, and received seven perfect marks.

BELOW: Time-sequence shot of Nadia Comaneci's perfect routine on the balance beam.

ABOVE: Bruce Jenner puts the shot on his way to the decathlon gold medal and a world-record 8,617 points.

ABOVE LEFT: Bruce Jenner finishing the 1,500 meters to wrap up his decathlon victory.

BELOW: John Naber's backstroke leg started the U.S. men's 400-meter medley relay team to the gold medal.

ABOVE: The U.S. women's 400-meter freestyle relay team celebrates after winning the gold medal in Montreal. Anchorwoman Shirley Babashoff is in the water; cheering on the deck are, from left, Wendy Boglioli, Kim Peyton and Jill Sterkel.

ABOVE: Teofilo Stevenson of Cuba won the heavyweight gold medal in Montreal, then repeated in Moscow four years later. Here, he's beating Romania's Mircea Simon in the Montreal final.

LEFT: Four years after the shock of Munich, the U.S. regained the men's basketball gold medal, beating Yugoslavia in the final with a team that included Bill Buckner (8), Steve Sheppard (5) and Phil Hubbard (14).

BELOW: Edwin Moses, arguably the greatest hurdler in history, winning the gold medal in the 400-meter hurdles in Montreal. Teammate Mike Shine was a distant second.

Juantorena was known as "White Lightning" for the all-white singlet, shorts and high socks of the Cuban team.

Kornelia Ender led the first big East German push in women's swimming. She won a record four gold medals as she and her teammates took all but two of the 13 women's swimming titles. The top U.S. swimmer, Shirley Babeshoff, set an Olympic record for frustration, with six silver medals behind Ender in the 1972 and '76 Games.

Klaus Dibiasi of Italy won his third consecutive gold medal in platform diving, coming from behind to beat a kid from America, Greg Louganis.

Lasse Viren of Finland repeated the double gold-medal feat of Munich, winning the 5,000 and 10,000 meters for an unprecedented four gold medals in the two events.

John Naber won four gold medals and Jim Montgomery three in swimming, where

American men took all but one of 13 golds. The only non-U.S. winner was David Wilkie of Britain, who won the 200-meter breaststroke.

Sugar Ray Leonard led a U.S. boxing team that also included future world champions Leon and Michael Spinks. Leonard, a good-looking, personable, talented fighter from the Washington, D.C., suburbs, became a TV star, gaining worldwide attention by taping a picture of his young son, Ray Jr., to his socks for inspiration in the ring.

Teofilo Stevenson of Cuba won his second of three consecutive boxing gold medals as a heavyweight. In his first three fights, Stevenson needed a total of 7 minutes, 22 seconds to wrap up the victories.

The United States regained the basketball gold medal, beating Yugoslavia in the final, 95-74. The team, which featured future NBA stars such as Phil Ford, Adrian Dantley and Walter Davis, almost lost in the early rounds to Puerto Rico, led by Marquette star Butch Lee, but hung on for a 95-94 victory.

LEFT: Alberto Juantorena of Cuba charges to victory in the 800 meters in Montreal, beating Belgium's Ivo Vandamme (103) and Rick Wohlhuter of the United States (970). Juantorena also won the 400.

BELOW: Stickers calling for a boycott of the Olympics that summer in Moscow were found around the 1980 Winter Games sites in Lake Placid, N.Y. The U.S. Olympic Committee eventually heeded President Carter's call for a boycott to protest the Soviet invasion of Afghanistan.

THE OLYMPICS AT 100

As the Games left Montreal, their future remained uncertain. The boycotts and the big debts had created doubts in the minds of governments, sports officials and fans over just what the Olympics was all about. Those doubts would grow in the next four years as the Olympics, once a haven from the world's problems, became the focal point in a battle of the superpowers.

Three days after Christmas in 1979, armies of the Soviet Union crossed the border into Afghanistan. Moscow said they had been "invited" to help stabilize the Afghan government. Much of the rest of the world saw it as an invasion to prop up a puppet in Kabul.

That view was held in the White House, and it would lead to the biggest Olympic boycott of all—and dramatic changes in the Games and the way they were run.

The IOC had awarded the 1980 Olympics to Moscow in the early 1970s. It was no great controversy, despite the raging Cold War. Soviet athletes had been back in the Games for more than two decades and had added much to the Olympic story. Administrators from the sports federations of the Soviet Union had taken on important duties in the IOC and other international groups. The nation was a superpower, and its capital of Moscow deserved the recognition of being an Olympic host.

Even though it was bound in an escalating struggle of ideologies with Moscow, the United States was planning to send a full team to the '80 Games. Funds were raised, team trials were scheduled and squads were being picked.

And then the tanks rolled into Afghanistan, and things changed.

President Jimmy Carter was outraged and wanted Americans to boycott the Moscow Games. The U.S. Olympic Committee didn't know what to do. It could follow the dictates of Avery Brundage, one of its own, and say the Olympics should stay out of politics. Or it could follow the voice of its nation's leader—a very loud voice, indeed, especially in a year in which Carter was facing re-election.

Finally, in the lobby of the Antlers Hotel in its headquarters city of Colorado Springs, Colorado, USOC officials announced that they had voted by a 2-to-1 margin to boycott the Games. Athletes, who had argued that the team should go to Moscow, were stunned; one of them, rower Anita DeFrantz, a medalist in Montreal, sued to have the decision overturned. The suit was unsuccessful. DeFrantz later became an IOC member.

NBC, which paid a record $72 million for the U.S. television rights, carried only tape-delayed highlights and filled its prime-time hours with regular programming.

Besides keeping U.S. athletes out, Carter wanted others to boycott, too. He called on U.S. allies around the globe to keep their teams home. Most Western countries concurred; some, such as Britain, urged their athletes to stay away but were overruled by their national Olympic committees.

In the end, 61 nations boycotted Moscow, while 81 others—including Afghanistan—attended. Some nations who did send teams decided to stage their own protests, such as marching under the Olympic flag or having the Olympic hymn played at medals ceremonies instead of their national anthems.

Stung by the boycott, the Soviets did all they could to make their Games memorable for other reasons. The stadiums and arenas they built were examples of socialist construction at its finest—big, utilitarian facilities, such as the 100,000-seat Lenin Stadium, comfortable enough but far from plush, capable of being used for track meets and Communist Party rallies. The total tab came to $9 billion, all of it in government money.

Security was tight and foreign visitors were limited in what they could see away from the events. Inside the stadiums, what they saw often looked strange. The Olympic flame was lit at opening ceremonies by Sergei Belov, whose third-try basket has beaten the United States in the

94

Munich gold medal game, and that choice of torchbearer proved to be prophetic.

The Moscow Games were marked by controversy over officiating—including a bizarre example in the men's triple jump. Two of the few Western athletes competing, Joao Carlos de Oliveira of Brazil and Ian Campbell of Australia, were called for fouls on nine of their 12 jumps. The gold and silver went to a pair of veteran Soviet athletes, Jaak Uudmae and Viktor Sanayev. Uudmae's winning leap was 56 feet, 11 ¼ inches, the same length as Saneyev had in winning his second of three consecutive gold medals in 1972 and almost 2 feet shorter than Oliveira's world record.

The Moscow Games featured the long-awaited middle-distance duel of Britain's Sebastian Coe and Steve Ovett, with Coe winning the 1,500 meters and Ovett the 800. But the Soviet Union, with athletes such as swimmer Vladimir Salnikov, dominated the Games, winning 80 of the 127 events and 195 medals overall. East Germany, its most powerful East bloc partner, was second with 47 golds and 126 medals.

ABOVE: In the 800 meters, Ovett held off a charging Coe to win the gold.

LEFT: Tiny Lake Placid attracted big crowds to its snowy streets for the 1980 Winter Games.

TOP: Sebastian Coe has a pained and shocked expression as he crosses the finish line to win the gold medal in the 1,500 meters in Moscow. His British teammate and archrival Steve Ovett (279) finished third, behind East Germany's Jurgen Straub.

95

LEFT: Eric Heiden swept the gold medals in all five men's speedskating events at Lake Placid. He's shown here en route to winning the last -- and longest -- of the bunch, the 10,000 meters.

ABOVE RIGHT: Hanni Wenzel of Liechtenstein won two skiing golds at Lake Placid, the slalom and the giant slalom.

RIGHT: The winningest racer in Alpine skiing history, Ingemar Stenmark of Sweden, got his only Olympic golds at Lake Placid, winning the men's slalom and giant slalom.

Ominously, the next Summer Olympics were to be held in the United States—in Los Angeles in 1984. The writing was on the wall: Expect a counter-boycott and more trouble for an already battered Olympic boat.

It was time for some deep soul-searching. And into this maelstrom stepped a quiet diplomat from Spain. Not much was known about him, but he would wind up saving the Olympics.

MIRACLE ON ICE

It's one of those special events, the kind that, years later, people remember exactly where they were when they heard the news.

The kind of event that stirs emotions and transcends sports.

The kind that people watch and don't quite believe.

A miracle. One carved out of ice.

The 1980 Winter Games were held in Lake Placid, New York, a sleepy little village in the Adirondacks. It was perfect for the Winter Games the first time it played host, in 1932. But by the time the '80 Winter Olympics started, it was clear that Lake Placid would be overwhelmed. It was, with massive foulups on tickets and transportation, and a Main Street so crowded on nights of competition it was hard to move.

The best thing about Lake Placid was the athletes.

American speedskater Eric Heiden won five gold medals in an unprecedented sweep of the men's distances. Hanni Wenzel of Liechtenstein won two gold medals in women's skiing, with Ingemar Stenmark of Sweden leading the men's skiers. Robin Cousins of Britain won the men's figure skating and Anett Potzsch of East Germany won the women's.

And the absolute saviors were a bunch of underdogs from Minnesota.

LEFT: Britain's Robin Cousins won the men's figure skating gold in '80.

BELOW: Goalie Jim Craig makes a spectacular save in the "Miracle on Ice" victory by the United States over the Soviet Union in Lake Placid.

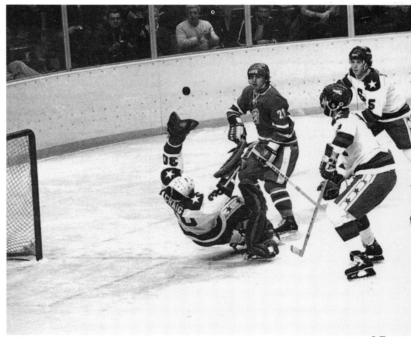

LEFT: The U.S. team used tight defense and rocket-like shots, such as this one, to beat the Soviets and then clinch the gold medal with a victory over Finland.

BELOW: The U.S. ice hockey team celebrates its 4-3 victory over the Soviets at Lake Placid, N.Y., in 1980.

ered to be the best hockey team in the world, the Soviet Union.

Tension between East and West was high. The Soviets had just sent troops into Afghanistan. The White House was calling for a boycott of the Moscow Olympics that summer. America was in the doldrums, standing by helplessly as Iranian students held more than 50 U.S. citizens—and by extension the entire nation—hostage in the embassy in Tehran.

The country needed a lift. Brooks and his boys sure gave it one.

The U.S. team tied Sweden in its first game 2-2 and then beat powerful Czechoslovakia 7-3. With a 7-2 win over Romania, the Americans were in the medal round.

The semifinal was against the Soviet Union, and most felt the run of success was about to end.

The Soviets were defending Olympic champions and reigning world champions. They had beaten a team of NHL all-stars 10-3 in an Olympic warmup match and taken the Americans apart 13-0. In the Olympic tournament, the Soviets won their first two games by a combined score of 33-4.

The semifinal between the two superpowers was played on a Friday afternoon. The ice hall, a small, 6,000-seat arena, was jammed, with scalpers doing a brisk business. This was home ice at its best, and the U.S. team responded.

Brooks told them to go out hard, and the Americans punished the Soviets with strong forechecking. Vladimir Krutov opened the scoring, but Buzz Schneider tied it 1-1. The Soviets led 2-1 on a goal by Sergei Makarov, before Mark Johnson made it 2-2 one second before the end of the first period. Aleksandr Maltsev put the Soviets ahead 3-2, and that's the way the second period ended. It was to be the last hurrah for the defending champions.

Johnson's second goal tied the game, and with 10 minutes remaining a 30-foot

The U.S. Olympic hockey team had been assembled seven months earlier. Herb Brooks, a young coach from the University of Minnesota, picked nine members from his college team and filled in the gaps with other players too young or too unskilled for the National Hockey League. The average age was 22.

In Innsbruck, the U.S. team finished fifth in the Olympics and was not given a chance of a medal in Lake Placid. Those would go, the experts said, to Canada, and Sweden. And, of course, the gold medal would go to what was generally consid-

slapshot by Mike Erizione, the team captain, put the United States ahead 4-3.

"U-S-A! U-S-A!" the crowd chanted. The seconds ticked down.

This was amazing! How could the young Americans beat the Soviets?

In the television booth, Al Michaels was handling play-by-play for ABC. The game would be telecast on tape-delay that night, but Michaels was playing it as if every man, woman and child in the United States was sitting right beside him.

As the last 20 seconds elapsed, the U.S. dumped the puck into the Soviet end one last time, and Michaels uttered a phrase that was truly gold-plated.

"Do you believe in miracles?" he asked the nation.

It did now.

The American team swarmed onto the ice as the final buzzer sounded. The Soviets couldn't believe it. The crowd made sure they knew it was no mirage.

In the locker room, the U.S. team sang "God Bless America." Two days later, it came from behind to beat Finland 4-2 for the gold medal, and the nation wrapped this team in the flag and in its hearts.

CHAPTER XI

President Samaranch

BELOW: Juan Antonio Samaranch, center, after his election as president of the International Olympic Committee in 1980. On the left is Lord Killanin, Samaranch's predecessor as IOC president.

His name is Juan Antonio Samaranch. His excellency, if you are a diplomat. The Marquis de Samaranch, if you pay attention to Spanish nobility.

You can call him "Stick."

That was the name this son of wealth used when he wrote a column on roller hockey for a newspaper in his hometown of Barcelona. Used to play goal for a local team, Samaranch did.

He still can stop the shots.

Samaranch became president of the International Olympic Committee in 1980, when the group and the Games were at perhaps their lowest ebb. He changed things right away, inserting business practices into what had been an old-boy network and deciding that money was not necessarily the evil some of his predecessors had declared it to be.

When Samaranch took over from Lord Killanin at the end of the Moscow Games, there was not much to hope for. The bank account was small and getting smaller. Two straight Summer Games had been hit by political boycotts, and a third was undoubtedly on the way. Groups such as the United Nations were seriously debating if they should take over the Olympics or perhaps set up their own international sports festivals, since this self-appointed group from Lausanne didn't seem capable of handling things in the modern world.

They hadn't counted on Samaranch, though, probably because they didn't know much about him.

"I'm always amazed at the ability we seem to have to pick the right person as our leader at just the right time," said Richard Pound, one of the IOC's most powerful members and a trusted Samaranch lieutenant. "We elected Samaranch and he realized it was time to get going. He made things happen."

Whether it knew what it needed or just got lucky, the IOC probably saved itself when it picked Samaranch overwhelmingly in balloting to succeed Killanin.

The son of textile and banking families in Barcelona, Samaranch had been a shadowy figure. He worked in family business, then became involved on regional levels in the fascist government of Francisco Franco, as documented by British journalists Vyv

Simson and Andrew Jennings in their 1992 book, *The Lords of the Rings*.

That is a time of his life that Samaranch prefers to avoid. During an interview in the late 1980s, for example, Samaranch was recounting some of the work he did prior to his IOC presidency. At one point, he was asked about a reference to "local government" work mentioned in his official IOC biography.

"I never worked in local government," he replied.

But it's on the biography sheet, the questioner persisted.

"That is wrong," Samaranch said. Next question.

When the Franco connection of that missing period was revealed in the Simson-Jennings book, Samaranch was furious and ordered a shakeup of the IOC's public relations operations, bringing in a high-priced spin-doctor to deflect such shots in the future. The IOC also sued—and won—in Swiss courts for criminal libel, although Simson and Jennings stood by their story.

Samaranch prefers to begin his life in the late 1960s, when he joined the IOC as a member from Spain. He worked his way up, holding increasingly powerful committee chairmanships, such as protocol and press relations. He was low-key but making contacts, among them Horst Dassler, the head of the Adidas athletic shoe and sportswear company. Dassler's connections and knowhow would prove invaluable to Samaranch.

In 1977, with the Franco regime long dead, Samaranch was assigned as the first Spanish ambassador to the Soviet Union. He used the time to meet people and learn what they wanted. And as the buildup to the Moscow Games—and the U.S.-led boycott—unfolded, he learned an awful lot about what makes the IOC tick.

"You must know very well what is your aim, what you are trying to get," Samaranch said. His aim was to make the Olympics a success. If that success, in turn, made others—such as Dassler—successful, that was OK, too.

Killanin's term was to expire in 1981, but he agreed to step down a year early so his successor could have additional time to plan for Los Angeles in 1984 and prepare for the difficulty that surely would lie ahead. Samaranch, with the help of the well-known and influential Dassler, lined up enough votes to easily defeat his challengers, who included Lance Cross of New Zealand and Willi Daume of West Germany.

Samaranch immediately said he would become a full-time president, the first in IOC history. He moved to Lausanne and set up shop, causing friction with Monique Berlioux, the IOC's administrator and de facto leader. Berlioux would have her powers steadily reduced and finally be fired in 1985.

The first thing that needed to be done, Samaranch felt, was to firm up the IOC's finances. The bank balance showed about $230,000, a pittance for an international organization. TV rights fees were rising, and could be expected to explode for Los Angeles. But most of that money went to local organizers or national Olympic committees. Samaranch changed that.

He directed that the IOC assume total control of television-rights negotiations and tightened the screws. NBC paid $87 million for Moscow, before boycott-related rebates; for LA in '84, IOC negotiators wangled a $225 million contract out of ABC.

The IOC gets 8 percent of the TV money. An equal percentage goes to what became the second part of Samaranch's platform of stability—Olympic Solidarity.

This program had been around for a while, providing money to sports programs in developing countries. But Samaranch saw it as a way to defuse political pressure on the Olympics. He decided to use Solidarity funds, now swollen with TV revenues, to pay for airfares, housing and living expenses for Olympic teams, if they could prove a need. For 1996, that will come to more than $25 million. And countries that boycott the Games are ineligible for Solidarity funding for four years.

Boycotts soon ended. And just as important, the money helped soothe relations between the various parts of the Olympic community, which used to resemble turf battles between rival gangs. Indeed, the cooperation that extends through most of he community is ranked by Samaranch as his greatest achievement.

"Sport has become very, very important," Samaranch said. "And the most important thing we have done is build unity. ... If we keep this unity, we can go very, very far."

Helping to build this unity was Samaranch's uncanny ability to disarm his enemies—not with a bludgeon, but with the velvet glove.

The IOC is one of the world's most prestigious clubs. It is self-appointed, it answers to no one, yet it has more direct contact and influence with governments and leading businesses worldwide than any other organization, including the UN. That kind of clout could produce jealousy among outsiders, but Samaranch succeeded in bringing potential plotters into the clubhouse.

It helps to be able to pay the bills, too, and that the IOC certainly can handle.

Virtually on the steps of the poorhouse when Samaranch took over, the IOC boasted assets at the close of 1993 of more than $125

LEFT: Samaranch at a Moscow news conference shortly after his election.

103

ABOVE: The Princess Royal greets Juan Antonio Samaranch during the opening ceremony of the Seoul Games in 1988.

million, with disposable funds of $76.8 million.

Sometimes, it seems as if Samaranch and other IOC leaders have become preoccupied with money, almost to the exclusion of sports. At times it feels as if "Richer, richer, richer" has replaced "Citius Altius Fortius" as the Olympic theme.

But Samaranch and the other argue that one of the reasons the IOC got into trouble two decades ago was a lack of money. And without funds, they say, the IOC cannot spread its gospel of peace and understanding through sports.

"These millions of dollars that are being funneled from the IOC to the third world and developing countries are to strengthen them, Olympic-wise," said John Lucas, a professor at Penn State University and a leading authority on the Olympic movement. "Therefore, Samaranch's preoccupation with money—and he is hugely preoccupied with money—is justifiable from his point of view because it enlarges the Olympic movement to embrace disenfranchised people who were never allowed to participate in the Olympics."

Sometimes, though, the money gets embarrassing, even to the IOC itself.

When it celebrated its own 100th birthday in 1994, the IOC staged a four-day Olympic Congress in Paris. Total cost: More than $30 million, with about half coming from its own bankbook and the rest from Parisian and French government funds.

Throughout the meeting, the IOC took great pains to show that the cost was in line with normal business conventions. It even did the unthinkable for this group of party animals—it threw just one party. The fact that it was a five-hour shindig of nonstop champagne and hors d'oeuvres for 3,000 of its closest friends did not faze the committee in the least.

In all the success, there are many places that critics can point to as possible cases where the Olympic rings have been corrupted. The immense amounts of money available to champion athletes have been blamed for the spread of performance-enhancing drugs. Businesses of the late Dassler have become quasi-official parts of the community. When the IOC decided to start a worldwide marketing program, TOP, in the late 1980s, for instance, the company picked to run it was ISL, a Swiss subsidiary of the Adidas empire. When Dassler died in 1986, many of those close to Samaranch said they had never seen him so sad.

What's more, the IOC can seem aloof and haughty. In Lillehammer for the Winter Games in 1994, many egalitarian Norwegians took offense at the limousines always waiting and the red carpets always spread for the IOC, and Samaranch did not receive the warmest reception.

But there can be no doubt that the Olympics are on solid footing now, and probably the most secure institution in the world. People are clamoring to stage the Games. The money comes rolling in. And athletes who once could only dream of Olympic participation are now taking part for real.

All of that is in large part thanks to Samaranch.

CHAPTER XII

I Love Los Angeles

BELOW: Peter Ueberroth in his Los Angeles Olympic office.

The news did not come as a surprise. Yet when it was announced, it still had a shock.

105

ABOVE: Greg Louganis flies off the 3-meter springboard en route to a gold medal in Los Angeles.

In May 1984, after months of avoiding the question, the Soviet Union announced that it was keeping its athletes home from that summer's Olympics in Los Angeles.

The stated reason was security. Moscow said it could not be sure its sons and daughters would be safe on the freeways and beaches of Southern California.

The real reason was revenge. The U.S.-led boycott of the Moscow Games in 1980 had hurt, and now it was time for a payback.

The IOC tried through sports and government channels to defuse the confrontation. By April, three months before the Games in LA would begin, it appeared as if all hope was lost. Committee President Juan Antonio Samaranch, in a last-ditch effort to save the Games from another boycott, arranged a meeting in Washington with President Ronald Reagan to try to win U.S.

government assurances that Soviet athletes would be welcome and safe.

The meeting was set for the White House the afternoon of May 8, 1984. That morning, Samaranch was due in New York for the start of the cross-country relay of the Olympic torch. As he prepared to leave for the capital, he got a phone call from one of his closest aides back in Lausanne.

Moscow had just announced the boycott.

"At first he said nothing," the aide recalled. "Then he just said, 'It will be all right.'"

That prediction was to prove eerily accurate.

A combination of good timing, great performances and unbounded patriotism helped turn the Los Angeles Olympics into the most successful sports event in history. It made a $230 million profit for American athletic training and support, showed the IOC how to make millions on its own and convinced the world that maybe these old Games were worth saving, after all.

In the end, most people didn't even miss the Soviet athletes or others who followed and heeded Moscow's call. Who needed Yuri and Natasha when we had Carl and Mary Lou?

The IOC had awarded the Games to Los Angeles in 1977, almost by default. There were no strong challengers, and even LA's candidacy was suspect. Alarmed by the billion dollars of red ink left over from the Montreal Games, voters in Los Angeles went better than 5-to-1 against spending a penny for Olympic-related projects.

The organizers, led by travel agency entrepreneur Peter V. Ueberroth, felt they could avoid the costliest part of staging a Games by using existing facilities. They would refurbish the Coliseum, which hosted the 1932 Games, and build two new venues—a cycling track and a swimming pool. Financing would come from an area largely untapped by the Olympics—commercial sponsors.

Go to a baseball stadium and you'll see scoreboards and outfield walls lined with billboards. Go to an Olympic event and you

LEFT: The form that helped Greg Louganis win four Olympic golds, here in the 3-meter springboard at Los Angeles.

BELOW: Swimming's "Madam Butterfly," Mary T. Meagher, churns up the Los Angeles pool in the 200 meters.

ABOVE: Indiana's Bobby Knight, U.S. Olympic basketball coach in 1984.

RIGHT: Michael Jordan goes up for a shot over a pick by Patrick Ewing as the U.S. team beats China. The future NBA stars led the United States to the gold medal.

won't see a single commercial sign inside the venue. IOC leaders like to say they save the arenas for the athletes; but by presenting a "clean" stadium, they also give unique platforms to businesses that tie on in other ways. Companies that buy ad time on Olympic telecasts, for instance, don't have to compete with another brand whose billboard is in camera range; firms that help build the Games get a one-of-a-kind "billboard," even if their name is nowhere to be seen.

That's what happened in Los Angeles. The velodrome was paid for by 7-Eleven, the swimming pool by McDonald's. Name recognition was sold to a limited number of sponsors in areas where quality was important—automobiles, cameras, copiers, airlines.

The financial base was there. ABC paid a record $225 million, almost three times the previous high, for U.S. rights fees. When

LEFT: The U.S. and Spain in basketball action in 1984.

ABOVE: Cheryl Miller, left, and Anne Donovan head upcourt following a turnover in the U.S. game against South Korea.

BELOW: Sebastian Coe completes an unexpected victory in the 1,500 meters in Los Angeles, becoming the first to successfully defend the gold medal at that distance.

ABOVE: A third-place finish in this heat gave Sebastian Coe (No. 359) a spot in the semifinal of the Los Angeles 1,500.

LEFT: Morocco's first Olympic gold medal was won in Los Angeles by Nawal El Moutawakil, waving the flag after her victory in the women's 400-meter hurdles.

BELOW LEFT: Daley Thompson powers through the long jump early in the decathlon competition. He won the gold medal in Los Angeles.

Moscow announced its boycott, ABC knew it didn't have to face the prospect its rivals at NBC had four years earlier, of pulling out of the Olympics.

ABC had been in Lake Placid for the "Miracle on Ice" hockey victory and seen first hand what success by American athletes could do to TV ratings.

An East-West showdown in LA could have been a big seller; the only problem when Good Guy meets Bad Guy is when Bad Guy wins, and that was always a possibility when U.S. and Soviet athletes met.

Once the Bad Guys eliminated themselves from Los Angeles, however, the focus was clear. ABC would make these America's Games.

There were plenty of U.S. stars to focus on. Carl Lewis was attempting to repeat Jesse Owens' feat of winning four gold medals in track. Greg Louganis was the world's best diver and expected to sweep

111

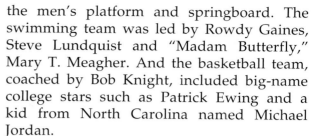

the men's platform and springboard. The swimming team was led by Rowdy Gaines, Steve Lundquist and "Madam Butterfly," Mary T. Meagher. And the basketball team, coached by Bob Knight, included big-name college stars such as Patrick Ewing and a kid from North Carolina named Michael Jordan.

It would be nice to have some foreign names, however, and the LA Games had an exotic mix. Britain's Seb Coe was back to try for a second straight gold medal in the 1,500; West Germany's Michael Gross, the "Albatross," was a fearsome sight in the men's swimming events. And for the first time since 1952, the world's biggest country, China, sent a team to the Olympics.

There were just enough East European names around to make the Los Angeles

ABOVE: Carl Lewis crosses the finish line first in the 100 meters in Los Angeles.

RIGHT: The king of the Los Angeles Games, Carl Lewis, waves the flag after his victory in the 100 meters.

ABOVE: Carl Lewis wins a heat of the men's 200 meters in 1984.

RIGHT: Evelyn Ashford wins the 100 meter race at the Los Angeles Olympics.

Games seem truly international. Moscow was unable to hold the line on some of its satellites, and Romania sent a particularly strong team.

They all were good stories. Coe won the 1,500 gold and gave the finger to British writers who had said he was over the hill. His teammate Daley Thompson swaggered to the decathlon title in a duel with West Germany's Juergen Hingsen. Gross set two world records and won two gold medals in the 100- and 200-meter butterfly. Said Aouita of Morocco won the 5,000 meters, and a teammate, Nawal El Moutawakel, won the women's 400-meter hurdles, the first female gold medalist from her country

113

and one of the first from any Muslim nation.

A Chinese shooter, Xu Haifong, won the first gold medal of the Games in the men's free pistol, touching off joyful street scenes in Beijing. In all, Chinese athletes won 15 gold medals.

Romania wound up second in the medals table, with 20 golds, 16 silvers and 17 bronze.

Day after day, night after night, from the rowing stadium at Lake Casitas north of the city to the wrestling arena in Long Beach far to the south, one song—"The Star-Spangled Banner"—topped the charts. And one cheer could be heard over and over and over, until it became almost nauseating: "U-S-A! U-S-A! U-S-A!"

Indeed, other nations complained to the IOC about the narrow minds of the fans and the narrow focus

RIGHT: Edwin Moses on his way to victory in the 400-meter hurdles.

BELOW: Carl Lewis (right), with Kirk Baptiste and Thomas Jefferson, take a victory lap with the American flag.

ABOVE LEFT: Joan Benoit wins the gold medal in the women's marathon at the Los Angeles Olympics.

ABOVE: Carl Lewis takes the baton from Calvin Smith in the 400 meter relay.

LEFT: Edwin Moses, with his wife, after winning the 400-meter hurdles.

RIGHT: Jeff Blatnick wins the gold for the U.S. in super heavyweight Greco-Roman wrestling.

BELOW: U.S. gymnast Bart Conner in action at the 1984 Olympics.

of ABC's telecasts. "Tell me, mate," Thompson asked at one point, "are there any other nations competing?"

But what could they do? Randy Newman had a hit record, "I Love LA," that summer, and American athletes kept calling for replays.

Lewis, who started his LA adventure with a wild news conference before escaping to a secret hideout in the Hollywood Hills, won his bout with Owens' ghost. He won the 100 meters, the 200, took the long jump while disdaining all but two of the six possible attempts, and capped the sweep with the anchor leg of the gold-medal 400-meter relay. Television focused on Lewis throughout the Games, but when that relay came, it was caught short. ABC showed prime-time viewers live action from preliminary rounds of diving, while Lewis and his teammates were passing the baton; it didn't get around to the historic relay until a later, tape-delayed segment.

Live or on tape, the show was red, white and blue. Evelyn Ashford duplicated Lewis' sprint triple, winning the women's 100 and 200 and anchoring the relay. Joan Benoit ran away with the first women's Olympic marathon. Meagher won the 100- and 200-meter butterflies, and U.S. swimmers took 21 gold medals. Jordan averaged 17 points a game and the U.S. men won the basketball gold medal by an average of 32 points a game; the women's team won gold as well, led by Cheryl Miller.

But there's no doubt that the absence of East bloc athletes helped the U.S. team more than anyone predicted.

Without Cuba, American boxers won nine gold medals, from light-flyweight Paul Gonzalez to super-heavyweight Tyrell Biggs.

Without East Germany, American cyclists won four gold medals, including the first

ABOVE: Bart Conner on the parallel bars.

LEFT: This hair-raising vault helped Mary Lou Retton to the women's all-around gymnastic gold medal in Los Angeles.

117

Above: Julianne McNamara during floor exercises in gymnastics competition.

Above Right: Julianne McNamara performs on the balance beam.

Right: U.S. gymnast Mary Lou Retton on the balance beam.

ABOVE AND RIGHT: Ecaterina Szabo performing on the balance beam in gymnastics competition.

ever by a woman, Connie Carpenter-Phinney, in the 50-mile road race.

Without the Bulgarians and Hungarians, American wrestlers won nine gold medals, including the super-heavyweight class in Greco-Roman with Jeff Blatnick. It was the second-biggest victory for Blatnick; he already had beaten cancer. "I'm a happy dude," he said, tears streaming down his face, after he decisioned Sweden's Thomas Johansson 2-0.

And without the Soviet Union, American gymnasts made history.

The men won the team championship for the first time, while the women took the silver. For the first time since 1932, an American man won an individual gymnastics gold, as Peter Vidmar tied Li Ning for first on the pommel horse and Bart Connor won the parallel bars.

All of this, in addition to Mary Lou Retton.

Coached by Bela Karolyi, who guided Nadia Comaneci to her historic "10" in Montreal, Retton was a 16-year-old from West Virginia when LA rolled around.

Bubbly, with a wall-to-wall smile and a penchant for gum and Corvettes, Retton was a made-for-TV teenybopper.

But could she win? Even with the Soviets absent, the women's field included the Romanians, who still had the best team in the world, and Ecaterina Szabo, probably the top individual gymnast.

Dressed in a red-white-and-blue leotard, Retton was ready to try. She won silver in the vault, bronze on the uneven bars and floor exercise, and joined with Julie McNamara, Tracee Talavera, Michelle Dusserre, Pam Bileck and Kathy Johnson for the team gold.

Retton started in gymnastics after being awed as an 8-year-old watching Comaneci perform on television from Montreal. Now she had her own chance to strut her stuff and perhaps inspire another generation of American gymnasts. But she needed to do something no American woman had done before: Win the Olympic all-around gold.

She and Szabo, a pair of 4-foot-9 giants, traded places at the top of the all-around standings through the first three events, with Szabo ahead by .05 points as they entered the last rotation. For Szabo, that was the uneven bars; for Retton, it was the vault.

Szabo went first and had what looked like a perfect routine until she staggered slightly on her dismount: 9.90. Retton needed 9.95 to tie, a perfect 10 to win.

"Now or never, OK?" shouted Karolyi. "OK," Retton shouted back.

The scene was Pauley Pavilion, where UCLA's basketball powerhouse was built. This time a little powerhouse ran down the runway, sprang from the takeoff board, soared with a twist over the padded back of the vaulting horse and landed like a nail struck by a sledgehammer, her feet never moving as they hit the mat.

"We did it," Retton shouted as her "10" was posted. Karolyi grabbed her in his arms.

Really, it was the only way the night—and the entire Olympics—could have ended.

This was America. Land of the free. Home of the gold.

LEFT: Mary Lou Retton celebrates after her balance beam performance at the Los Angeles Games. She became the first American woman to win an individual Olympic gold medal in gymnastics.

ABOVE: Olympic gymnasts Mary
Lou Retton and Peter Vidmar.

RIGHT: Katarina Witt finishes with
a smile and a spin for the
women's figure skating gold
medal in Sarajevo.

Above: This child may not
have agreed, but Vucko the
Wolf was the friendly mascot
of the 1984 Winter Games in
Sarajevo.

CHAPTER XIII

Olympics New Era

BELOW: IOC President Juan Antonio Samaranch (left) and Park Seh-jik of the Seoul Olympic Organizing Committee at the unveiling ceremony of a bronze statue donated by Samaranch.

L os Angeles might have been chauvinistic. It might have lacked some of the world's best athletes. It might have been impossible to stage in any other city, at any other time.

But the Los Angeles Games showed that the Olympics could be run on a shoestring—the total budget was less than $500 million—while making money through private sponsorships. And it showed that the time for Olympics boycotts was over.

The next Games would be in Seoul in 1988, and thus that last lesson would prove to be the most important.

The IOC has chosen Seoul over Nagoya, Japan, in voting in 1981. It was a surprise. South Korea was just emerging as an economic power on the Pacific Rim and technically still at war with North Korea. This was in the heyday of the Cold War, and no place was chillier than the demilitarized zone between the two countries, just 35 miles north of Seoul.

The vote was announced by IOC President Juan Antonio Samaranch in his usual, matter-of-fact tones, without a flinch. In subsequent years, as one crisis after another burst on Seoul's Olympic preparations, Samaranch would maintain that the IOC had picked the right city. "I said at the time the choice was the correct one, and I still support that decision," was the party line from the IOC boss.

But when Samaranch opened the envelope on September 29, 1981, and saw the winner's name, he actually had much different thoughts: "What have we done?"

Having just weathered the Moscow boycott and preparing, at least subconsciously, for retaliation in 1984 in Los Angeles, Samaranch knew that his road—and the IOC's—was not about to get any easier.

Indeed, the next seven years would be among the busiest of his life. In the end, they would also be the most successful.

Soon after the vote, North Korea—also a member of the IOC—began making noises of displeasure. Shortly before the 1984 Games, the first sign of definite action came, with top officials in Pyongyang suggesting a boycott unless their interests were served. It wasn't long before the idea of placing some Olympic events in North Korea was broached.

Richard Pound, an IOC vice president who related Samaranch's thoughts on the vote in his book, *Five Rings Over Korea*, wrote that the split-Games idea may have originated in one of two high-ranking government spots: Either from Italian Foreign Minister Julio Andreotti or Cuban Premier Fidel Castro.

Whatever the source of the idea, North Korean officials started pressing the IOC and threatening to lead a boycott if they were ignored. By late 1985, Samaranch called the two Koreas together in the first of what would be four meetings to discuss dividing the Games.

Whether there ever was any way the 1988 Games could have been held north and south of the DMZ may never be known. Olympics are awarded to cities, not countries, and the only time they have been split was in 1956, when Australian quarantine laws forced equestrian events to be held in Sweden.

And whether North Korea ever had any intention of agreeing to any IOC proposal and thus participating in the land of its fiercest enemy can be debated endlessly. Certainly, whatever plans the IOC put forward—from hosting certain events to running a cycling race across the border to allowing an IOC delegation to travel directly from Pyongyang to Seoul—eventually were rejected by the North. But agreeing to sit down and discuss the matter was Samaranch's masterstroke.

"The door is always open," he kept saying, as proposal after proposal was turned down and the opening ceremonies in Seoul got closer and closer.

Seoul had been awarded the Games, and the IOC was not about to renege on that commitment. What Samaranch wanted to make sure of was the participation of as many nations as possible, including China, the Soviet Union and others who might support the Communist North Korean regime.

He did it. Through four years and two million miles of air travel, Samaranch brought the Olympic family together again.

LEFT: U.S. swimmer Janet Evans on her way to a win in a preliminary 400-meter freestyle race at the Seoul Olympics.

LEFT: U.S. swimmer Janet Evans on her way to a win in a preliminary 400-meter freestyle race at the Seoul Olympics.

BELOW: Janet Evans smiles after her gold-medal performance in the women's 400-meter medley.

He was helped by changing attitudes in the East and West, and the rapid emergence of South Korea as both a manufacturer and consumer.

By late 1987 and early '88, many East bloc countries were looking at Seoul as the provider of consumer goods and a market for their own products. Trade missions were established, even between South Korea and Moscow. The Cold War was melting, and the Olympics would be one of the first beneficiaries.

In September 1987, invitations were sent to IOC member countries asking them to send their athletes to Seoul in one year. This was another strategic ploy by Samaranch, much like the usurping of TV rights negotiations. Previously the invitations went out from host committees; if the IOC issued them, Samaranch reasoned, it would be harder for countries to reject them for political reasons.

Above: The U.S. 4x100 meter medley team celebrates their world-record gold medal performance at Seoul in 1988. (Left to right: Matt Biondi, David Berkoff, Richard Schroeder and —in water—Christopher Jacobs.

The door stayed open until the last minute. And in the end, 160 nations and 9,421 athletes took part in Seoul. North Korea stayed away, along with Cuba, Ethiopia and Nicaragua.

"Nobody wins in boycotts," said Vitaly Smirnov, who—as an IOC member from the Soviet Union—had felt the pain of two big ones.

Trying to get all of the world's nations to Seoul was a massive job for the IOC, but these Games had more hurdles to overcome.

At least two fatal bombings—one at Kimpo International Airport prior to the 1986 Asian Games, the other aboard a Korean Airlines flight over Burma in 1988 that killed 115 people—were linked by South Korean investigators to North Korean attempts to disrupt the Games.

The buildup to the Olympics accompanied the transition of South Korean government from military dictatorship to democracy. And that change was accompanied by repeated clashes between police and demonstrators in Seoul's downtown and university areas. Fighting became so violent in 1987 that there was speculation the Games would be canceled or moved; the IOC found it necessary to state that only war could force the Games to be changed.

Against all this social and political upheaval, actually building the stadiums for the Olympics may have been among the easiest tasks the Koreans faced. And they pulled the task off in splendid fashion, converting wasteland on the south bank of the Han River into two parks filled with Olympic venues, including the main stadium that evoked an ancient Korean flower bowl. In all, the projects cost a staggering $3.1 billion.

Virtually all the nations of the world and all the top athletes were on hand when giant drums and dragon chants opened the Seoul Games on September 17, 1988.

Stars to be crowned included Janet Evans and Matt Biondi, the leaders of a strong American swim team. Evans won three gold medals while Biondi—who some predicted would match Mark Spitz's record seven golds—won five golds, a silver and a bronze. Kristin Otto of East Germany won six gold medals, the most ever by a female swimmer.

There was Greg Louganis, banging his head on the springboard and requiring stitches to close the cut, yet finishing his Olympic career with two more gold medals. (Seven years later, Louganis revealed in an autobiography that he was suffering from AIDS and knew he had the AIDS virus at the time he hit his head and bled in the Olympic pool. He didn't tell the doctor who stitched him up, even though that physician

ABOVE: East Germany's Kristin Otto at the start of the 100-meter backstroke event she won at the Seoul Olympics, capturing a gold medal.

RIGHT & FAR RIGHT: U.S. diver Greg Louganis hitting his head on the springboard during preliminary dives at the Olympics in Seoul.

LEFT: Jackie Joyner-Kersee (center) after winning the gold medal in the heptathlon at the Seoul Olympics. Silver winner Sabine John (left) and bronze winner Anke Behmer, both of East Germany, share the podium.

BELOW: Jackie Joyner-Kersee in the shotput phase of the heptathlon.

RIGHT: Florence Griffith-Joyner celebrates her victory in the 100-meter dash at the 1988 Olympics.

Above: U.S. sprinter Florence Griffith-Joyner strides to a world record in a semifinal heat of the 200 meters in Seoul.

was not wearing protective gloves.) Jackie Joyner-Kersee finally won the heptathlon gold that eluded her in Los Angeles, and the United States won the men's volleyball gold medal with an unbeaten record. The U.S. men's basketball team, however, managed only a bronze medal, as the Soviet Union beat Yugoslavia for the gold. It would be the last Olympics in which the United States would send college players onto the basketball court.

The competition was fierce and the memories lasting. Yet the legacy of Seoul was one of disgrace.

Drug use to hype performance had been around for decades. Officials acknowledged it, and instituted doping tests to try to stop it. But the athletes always seemed to be one step ahead of the testers, learning newer and better ways to hide that lightning they carried in their bottles.

Ben Johnson was one of that group. A Jamaican native who moved with his family to Toronto as a child, Johnson was a short, compact man who liked to run fast. He was a member of the Canadian bronze-medal relay team in Los Angeles in 1984, but not considered anything special.

All of a sudden, he was very special. A new, improved Ben Johnson appeared, muscles bulging and eyes the color of lemonade. And wherever Johnson ran, records began to fall.

LEFT: U.S. Olympic basketball coach John Thompson walks off dejectedly after a loss to the Soviets.

BELOW: Canadian Ben Johnson (arm raised, third from left) looks over at rival Carl Lewis (No. 102) at the finish line of the 100-meter race in Seoul.

ABOVE: Ben Johnson of Canada leading in the 100-meter dash at the Seoul Olympics. American Carl Lewis finished second and Linford Christie of Great Britain was third.

LEFT: Ben Johnson sets a world record and wins a gold medal in the 100 meter dash.

It's not unusual for two track athletes to dodge each other in the regular season. A loss in a run-of-the-mill meet can cost an athlete thousands of dollars in future appearance money and endorsements. So sprinters like Johnson and Lewis only challenge each other at the majors, and the next major was the Seoul Olympics.

"When the gun go off," Johnson said, "the race be over."

The buildup to the 100 in Seoul was like the buildup to a heavyweight fight or a Hollywood premiere. The two athletes challenged and prodded each other, and through the heats Lewis was just slightly faster—but Johnson looked as if he had something in reserve.

Track in Seoul did not always draw capacity crowds. But for the 100 final, you couldn't find a ticket. The stadium was packed. Johnson was in lane 6, Lewis in lane 3. They crouched in their starting blocks.

The gun went off. The race was over.

Johnson, a fast starter, was faster than ever. He exploded from the blocks and just pulled away, glancing over his left shoulder at the beaten Lewis and thrusting the No. 1 sign in the air as he crossed the finish line. The time: 9.79, another world record. Lewis was second in 9.92, and the first four finishers all broke 10 seconds. Johnson had confirmed his title as the world's fastest human and was declared a "national treasure" back home.

That night, the drug lab began work on Johnson's urine sample, collected with some difficulty after the race. Johnson was dried out from the exertion and tension, and had to drink several beers before he would urinate. What the lab found was more than malt and hops. Johnson had been using stanozolol, an anabolic steroid.

Olympic drug tests are done in two parts. When the first part of Johnson's was finished, it was reported to the IOC, which matched the code number on the test with the athlete's name. It called the Canadian

In Rome, at the World Track and Field Championships in 1987, Johnson ran his first big duel with Carl Lewis. On a hot Sunday afternoon in the 100-meter finals, he blew away Lewis and the world record, lowering it to 9.83 seconds—.09 seconds lower than the previous mark.

Lewis and other competitors had been hinting for some time that Johnson was on drugs—steroids, to be precise. They help the body rebound from injury, and when you run as fast as Johnson you basically injure yourself with every stride. Ben swore he was clean and indeed passed all the drug tests. He kept running and winning.

THE OLYMPICS AT 100

RIGHT: Olympic champion Katarina Witt of East Germany mimics Michael Jackson at the figure skating exhibition in Calgary in 1988.

delegation, which would be present when the second part of the test was conducted.

That test came back positive, too. Big Ben had been busted. He was the 40th athlete to flunk an Olympic drug test, but he was by far the biggest name.

To avoid the hubbub of the Olympic village, Johnson, like a lot of top athletes, had moved to a Seoul hotel, checking in under the name "John Benson." Armed with the test results, Canadian Olympic officials went to Johnson's room—to get his gold medal back, and to tell him goodbye.

"We love you," Canadian team leader Carol Ann Letheren told the sprinter, "but you're guilty."

Johnson's disgrace led to a government probe of drug use by Canadian athletes, at which he testified he was on steroids when he set the world record in Rome. Track's governing body, the International Amateur Athletic Federation, later stripped Johnson of that title and world record, even though he passed the drug test there. After a two-year suspension, he ran in the 1992 Games, but later flunked another drug test and was banned again.

The Olympic gold medal went to Lewis. A year earlier, the American star had placed his gold medal from the 100 in Los Angeles in the casket of his father, who had died of cancer. The night Johnson was kicked out of Seoul, Lewis, a devout Christian, was a guest preacher at a Baptist church near the Olympic stadium.

"After the race the other day, I dreamed my father came to me," Lewis told the congregation. "And he said, 'Don't worry. Everything will be all right.'

"And now," Lewis said with a smile, "we know it is."

ABOVE: An arrow carrying the Olympic flame leaves the bow of archer Antonio Rabollo to light the Olympic torch in Barcelona.

BELOW: Doves, symbolizing peace, are released in the Olympic Stadium in Barcelona during opening ceremonies.

CHAPTER XIV

Barcelona 1992

W hat if they held an Olympics and everybody came?

Not just some athletes—the best, from every country.

And what if that meant the best, whether they were amateurs or professionals? Would that be a party or what?

That's just about what happened in Barcelona in the summer of 1992, when the Olympics truly did become a festival of the world's youth, and nobody had to check their bankbooks at the door.

Pros had been in the Games since 1984, and the tennis players in 1988 in Seoul showed that even the richest could live in the Olympic Village and enjoy it.

But some of the world's best were still barred. That included a group that the United States yearned to get into the Games—its best basketball players, the multimillion-dollar stars of the NBA.

The door was opening for some time, since the upset of the all-amateur U.S. team in 1972. It accelerated after the bronze-medal finish in Seoul. And by the following spring, Magic and Bird and Michael were being measured for warmup suits with USA on the front.

In April 1989, FIBA, the international basketball federation, met in Munich—the site of the 1972 loss—to debate whether to open its world championships and Olympic tournament to pros. The Soviet Union was

ABOVE: Performers with flares run across the field at opening ceremonies in Barcelona.

PREVIOUS PAGE: A giant mechanical Hercules is wheeled out for rehearsals of the opening ceremonies in Barcelona.

against the move and carried a lot of power in FIBA, and passage of the measure was uncertain. If it did, the U.S. officials knew, they would have no excuses if they failed to win gold medals for some time to come.

"If they pass this rule," Dave Gavett, the secretary general of USA Basketball, said the night before the vote, "I guarantee the gold medal in Barcelona. No ifs, ands or buts."

The next day, FIBA adopted the rule change—Gavett, reflecting the interests of high school, college and other amateur groups in his federation, was one of the few delegates to vote against it—and the Olympics in essence made the final transition from the amateur days of Coubertin to the days when all the best were welcomed.

"Sometimes," Gavett said, "they just put the puck on your stick."

Thus begot the "Dream Team"—Magic Johnson, Larry Bird, Michael Jordan, Patrick Ewing, Chris Mullin, John Stockton, Karl Malone, Scottie Pippen, Charles Barkley, Clyde Drexler and David Robinson. NBA All-Stars, every one of them. Christian Laettner, the best player in college ball that year, was thrown in for good measure.

Never had there been a basketball team—or perhaps *any* team—assembled for international competition that was quite this good. The rest of the world knew it. They were playing for silver; the highlight for most opponents was just to be on the same court with these guys, and most made sure they had their pictures taken with the U.S. squad once the rout was over.

The toughest job for U.S. coach Chuck Daly, who had two NBA titles of his own with Detroit, was finding enough minutes in the games to keep all his all-stars happy. He did a masterful job, and the Dream

ABOVE: Basketball coach Chuck Daly with the U.S. team in Barcelona.

PREVIOUS PAGE: Earvin "Magic" Johnson drives past an Angolan defender in a preliminary round victory for the U.S. in Barcelona.

PREVIOUS PAGE: Michael Jordan soars high above teammate Magic Johnson to knock away a shot during a preliminary round game against Croatia.

THIS PAGE: Magic Johnson waves the U.S. flag in celebration during the gold medal ceremony for the U.S. basketball team.

LEFT: Teresa Edwards of the U.S. defends a pass from Spain's Daedra Charles while both are on their knees in a women's basketball game in Barcelona.

BELOW: Britain's Sally Gunnell (right) on her way to winning the 400-meter hurdles. Sandra Farmer-Patrick of the U.S. won the silver.

Team was an artistic success, averaging 127.3 points a game and winning by an average of 43.8. It never scored less than 100 points, and it never allowed an opponent near 90. The closest outcome—a 32-point victory over Croatia in the gold-medal game.

Will there ever be a better team, Johnson, the captain, was asked.

"Maybe," said Magic, then 33, "but none of us will be around to see it."

Great? Undoubtedly. Olympian? Well ...

"We do not want sport to become just entertainment," said Vitaly Smirnov, a member of the IOC from the Soviet Union, who helped to open the Games to professionals. "When you go to the Bolshoi to see *Swan Lake*, you already knows who lives and dies. That is why we love sport. The outcome is not known in advance."

In Barcelona, who would win the basketball gold might have been the only thing that was a sure thing.

The city of Picasso, Miro and Gaudi had used the Games to revitalize itself. It took a dilapidated port and turned it into beautiful beachfront. Rail lines were replaced by apartments for athletes with a view of the Mediterranean. The old stadium on the top of Montjuic, a remnant of pre-Franco days, was gutted and turned into a state-of-the-art facility for track. A stunning 20,000-seat arena for gymnastics was built next door.

Highways were constructed, rail lines rerouted and the airport brought up to date. Some $8 billion in all were spent on the Olympics and related projects.

But the question was, would it work? Barcelona was an expensive, iconoclastic place to visit or do business in. How would this capital of Catalonia take to the Games?

Stupendously.

Every night, the Ramblas, Barcelona's Fifth Avenue, pulsed with excitement. And so did the stadiums and arenas. Barcelonans and their visitors turned the venues and the

ABOVE: From left: Maria de Lurdes Mutola of Mozambique, Inna Yevseyeva of the Unified Team, Joetta Clark of the U.S., and Lili Nurutdinova of the Unified Team qualifying for the 800-meter final in Barcelona.

147

LEFT: Jamaica's Merlene Ottey wins the first heat of the 100 meters in Barcelona.

BELOW: Esther Jones (right) hands baton to U.S. teammate Carlette Guidry in the 4 x 100 meter relay in Barcelona.

Gail Devers. The American sprinter suffered from Grave's disease, a debilitating blood disorder that almost forced doctors to amputate her feet. Those feet, now healed, carried her to the gold medal in the women's 100 meters and just missed winning the 100 hurdles when she fell while leading in the final strides.

Carl Lewis. Ill with a virus during the U.S. trials, the veteran qualified in the long jump and won for a third straight Olympics.

Paraskevi Patoulidou. When Devers fell, Patoulidou sped by, with the first gold medal by a Greek woman in track and field.

Evelyn Ashford. The triple-gold medalist in LA, she won her fifth Olympic gold for the United States in the women's 400-meter relay.

Alexandr Popov. A member of the Unified Team, he won the two fastest swimming races, the men's 50- and 100-meter freestyles.

Yael Arad. Her silver medal in women's half-middleweight judo was the first ever won by an Israeli athlete.

Vitali Scherbo. A native of Belarus, Scherbo competed for the Unified Team and dominated men's gymnastics, winning six gold medals. On the last night of the competition, as he won golds on the vault, parallel bars, pommel horse and rings, Scherbo wore the hammer-and-sickle symbol of the Soviet Union. It wasn't a political statement, he explained. He was just saying thanks to the system that made him a champion.

surrounding neighborhoods into big sports parties. Lasers pierced the sky above the old royal palace as the athletes put on their show.

And what a show! With no boycott this time—no reason to—you had to be the absolute best to be an Olympic champion.

For the first time since 1952, German athletes competed as one team. South Africa was back, its international banishment ended by the fall of apartheid. The Soviet Union had split up with the end of Communist rule, but the IOC worked a deal allowing most of its former republics to be represented as a Unified Team, to save training and other expenses. And strings were pulled and loopholes found to permit athletes from Yugoslavia, on the world's blacklist for aiding the rampage through its former republic of Bosnia, to compete under the Olympic flag.

In all, 10,563 athletes from a record 172 nations took part. That's 10,252 more athletes than competed in Athens in 1896. Some of the best:

The home team had extra incentive. In keeping with the Dream Team motif, Spain offered $1 million to any of its athletes who won a gold medal. A record 13 Spaniards did it—more than four times the number of gold medals Spain had produced in all the previous Olympics combined!

Now, THAT'S a dream come true.

LEFT: Jackie Joyner-Kersee makes her second shot put in the Olympic heptathlon in Barcelona.

BELOW: The three medalists in the Barcelona decathlon, from left: Spain's Antonio Penaluer (silver), Czechoslovakia's Robert Zmelik (gold) and American Dave Johnson.

PREVIOUS PAGE, TOP: From left: Evelyn Ashford, Esther Jones, Gwen Torrence and Carlette Guidry celebrate the U.S. victory in the 4 x 100 meter relay.

PREVIOUS PAGE, BOTTOM: The U.S. women's 4 x 100 relay team, after winning the gold at the Barcelona Olympics. From left: Gwen Torrence, Carlette Guidry, Esther Jones and Evelyn Ashford.

LEFT: U.S. sprinter Dennis Mitchell breaks from the starting blocks in a heat of the 100-meter dash.

BELOW: Carl Lewis during his third jump in the long jump finals in Barcelona.

ABOVE: Competitors jump over the hurdle at the water jump during the 3,000-meter steeplechase.

TOP PHOTO: Canada's Mark McKoy (right) wins the gold in the 110-meter hurdles. Jack Pierce of the U.S. (left) finished third and Germany's Florian Schwarthoff finished fifth.

ABOVE: Track events are the most popular of the Summer Olympics, this race taking place in Barcelona in 1992.

BELOW: Sprinting to the finish line on the anchor leg of a heat in the 4 x 400 meter relay.

ABOVE: The USA men's 4 x 100 meter relay team carry American flags as they celebrate a world record win at Barcelona. From left: Carl Lewis, Mike Marsh, Leroy Burrell, and Dennis Mitchell.

ABOVE: Great Britain's Steve Backley, who won the bronze, makes his third toss in the javelin competition.

RIGHT: Rosen Nahum of Israel competes in the triple jump.

LEFT: A wrestling clinch by Abdollah Chamangoli of Iran (left) and Germany's Claudio Passarelli in the Olympic 68k class.

BELOW: China's Li Xiaosahuang pushes off the pommel horse during the individual all-around event. He finished fifth.

LEFT: Vitaly Scherbo of the Unified Team performs on the pommel horse during gymnastic finals in Barcelona. The Unified Team won the gold.

BELOW: American Dominick Minicucci approaches the horse during vaulting competition.

158

ABOVE: Romania's Lavinia Corina Milosovici during the floor exercises in gymnastics competition. She scored a 10 and won the gold at Barcelona.

RIGHT: Elena Groudneva of the Unified Team performing on the balance beam.

ABOVE: Fernando Gandolfi shoots on goal to give Italy an overtime water polo victory over Spain and a gold medal.

LEFT: Pablo Morales of the U.S., after winning the 100-meter butterfly at the Barcelona Olympics.

BELOW: Californian Pablo Morales on his way to the gold in the 100-meter butterfly. Poland's Rafal Szukala (behind) took the silver.

ABOVE: USA's Anita Nall on her way to victory in the 200-meter breaststroke, beating out Kyoko Iwasaki of Japan.

RIGHT: U.S. swimmer Matt Biondi dives in to start a heat of the 50 meter freestyle.

BELOW: Martin Lopez-Zubero of Spain leaps into the water on his way to the gold medal in the 200-meter backstroke.

U.S. figure skater Nancy Kerrigan during the free skating program at the Winter Olympics in Albertville, France.

CHAPTER XV

ABOVE & BELOW: Britt Pedersen (right) hands the Olympic torch to ski-jumper Stein Gruben, who went down the ski jump during opening ceremonies in Lillehammer in 1994.

Lillehammer 1994

I t started with a whack to the knee. "Why me?" Nancy Kerrigan wailed. "Why now?"

ABOVE: Children prepare to form the Olympic rings at the opening ceremony of the Lillehammer Olympics.

Kerrigan was the silver medalist in women's figure skating at the 1992 Winter Olympics and was among the favorites to win the gold medal two years later, when the Winter Games would be held in Lillehammer, Norway, for the first time on a new schedule.

She was preparing for the U.S. National Figure Skating Championships in Detroit in January, about six weeks before the Olympics, when a man ran up to her beside a practice rink and hit her hard on the right knee with a metal bar. He escaped by using his head to crash through a locked Plexiglas door.

Kerrigan wound up with a bad bruise and a seat in a skybox for the women's national championship. The title would go to Tonya Harding, her archrival.

Both would skate in Lillehammer. But in between, they would become involved in one of the most bizarre stories in Olympic history, a criminal "hit" by one athlete on another.

To begin, let's go back eight years, to the shores of Lake Geneva.

The IOC's annual meeting in 1986 was held in its headquarters city of Lausanne, Switzerland. The prime topic was selection of the host cities for the Summer and Winter Games in 1992, but there was something else on the agenda that would have a more far-reaching impact.

Winter sports weren't officially recognized by the IOC until 1920, when figure skating and ice hockey were held as part of the summer program in Antwerp. By the next Games, in 1924, cold-weather countries and sports had persuaded the IOC to stage a separate Winter Games. Coubertin, the IOC's founder, was not thrilled, but the Winter Olympics became a part of the regular four-year calendar.

The IOC was based in Switzerland, with a view of some of the highest mountains and best skiing snow in the world, but for some reason its leaders kept the Winter Games at arm's length. Avery Brundage, for one, despised them, and said at one point that he hoped they would be given "a proper burial."

But the Winter Games provided some of the greatest moments in Olympic history, such as Franz Klammer's banzai run to win the 1976 downhill in Innsbruck, or the U.S. hockey team's "Miracle on Ice" at Lake Placid in 1980, or the fiery *Bolero* in ice dancing by Jayne Torvill and Christopher Dean in Sarajevo in 1984, or the duelling "Carmens" of figure skaters Katarina Witt and Debi Thomas in 1988.

Television loved the Winter Games. It was ready-made programming for a time of year when people were practically captive

audiences, and the sports—especially figure skating—produced higher and higher ratings.

Marketing managers found that sponsors liked the Winter Games, too. But like TV, they had a problem: Not enough money in their annual budgets to spend on both the Winter and Summer Olympics in the same year.

Having discovered the sweet smell of cash in Los Angeles, the IOC looked for ways to ease more money out of the bank accounts of multinational companies and TV networks. And it found the answer in the calendar.

Nothing in the rules said the Summer and Winter Games had to be in the same year. It was a tradition, but the IOC had found that tradition doesn't pay the bills. It was time for a change.

It would not touch the Summer Games. But beginning in 1994, the IOC decided, the Winter Games would be on their own quadrennial cycle. And that gave athletes a one-time shot at doubling their Olympic fun.

It's coincidence, but the prime of most athletic careers is about three years. That

ABOVE: U.S. skater Nancy Kerrigan addresses the media outside her Massachusetts home, answering questions about the assault on her.

RIGHT: Jeff Gillooley, ex-husband of figure skater Tonya Harding, after meeting with investigators in connection with the Nancy Kerrigan assault case.

RIGHT: Jeff Gillooley, ex-husband of figure skater Tonya Harding, after meeting with investigators in connection with the Nancy Kerrigan assault case.

means that, for most athletes, it's one shot at a gold medal and then goodbye. Placing the Lillehammer Games just two years after the Albertville Olympics provided a once-in-a-lifetime opportunity for any athlete who felt they could scrimp and save just a little while longer in the quest for Olympic glory.

That appealed to both Kerrigan and Harding, Olympic teammates in '92. Both failed to win the big prize that would guarantee million-dollar contracts with ice shows, sponsors and TV networks. It was on to Lillehammer.

Kerrigan and Harding were both world-class skaters but as different as they could be in style and personality.

Kerrigan was the more traditional image of an ice princess. Tall and willowy, with long dark hair, she reminded some of a young Katharine Hepburn. She lived with her parents in a Boston suburb and was very close to her mother, who was legally blind and had to sit within inches of a television screen to see her daughter perform. Her skating was stylish and smooth; not a great jumper, she compensated with quick footwork and complete routines.

Harding was an outsider. She came from the poor side of town in the suburbs of Portland, Oregon, the product of a broken home and an abusive mother. She smoked, drank beer, shot pool and drove a pickup truck. She met her ex-husband, Jeff Gillooley, as a 15-year-old, and the relationship had its ups and downs. Harding had left Gillooley at least once and there were police reports of domestic violence.

So the two skaters went to Detroit, where Nancy got whacked and Tonya won. Kerrigan went back to Boston to rehab, and hope to win a special dispensation from U.S. Figure Skating for a berth on the Olympic team. Harding returned to Portland and almost immediately was faced with some tough questions.

Authorities were tipped that the assailant had been hired to attack Kerrigan, to knock her out of the Nationals and the Olympics so Harding could win. The trail started with Shawn Eckhardt, a 310-pound friend of Gillooley's and a would-be bodyguard for the skater. He convinced two friends, Shane Stant and Derrick Smith, that they all could make big money providing security services to skaters, but first the skaters had to feel there was reason to be scared. They targeted Kerrigan. It took a while for Stant to track her down, but he finally caught up with her in Detroit and let her have it on the knee.

The trouble was, the blow wasn't hard enough to do permanent damage. Kerrigan recovered and made the Olympic team. And Eckhardt started talking, first telling his story to a minister who passed it to the police.

From Eckhardt, Stant and Smith, the threads led to Gillooley, and then quickly to Harding. With the Olympics approaching,

reports grew heavier and heavier that Harding had been involved in plotting the attack to remove her chief rival, then helped cover up the crime once it was done.

The skater and her husband denied any knowledge. But prosecutors in Multnomah County, Oregon, pressed on and struck a deal with Gillooley, who implicated Harding in a plea bargain. A court hearing Feb. 1, just 11 days before the Olympics began, heard Ron Hoevet, Gillooley's lawyer, call for Harding to resign from the team. "The truth about this bizarre crime has now been revealed," he said.

Harding continued to deny knowledge of the crime, although she acknowledged that he had not told investigators everything she did know right away. She insisted she would skate in Lillehammer.

Others started thinking differently.

The U.S. Figure Skating Association had control over the Olympic figure skating team until that roster was handed to the U.S. Olympic Committee. Figure skating officials were upset about the reports and testimony implicating their national champion in a crime against a teammate. But there were no charges yet, and officials were fearful any moves they made would be met with a lawsuit.

It was especially frustrating because the skater was Tonya Harding. Others had come from blue-collar backgrounds to become skating champions. But Harding contradicted all the assumptions about a champion skater, and retained that rough edge.

The USOC insisted that its own rules barred it from acting until the federation submitted its roster. Privately, it was seething, and wanted to kick Tonya off the team. But it couldn't take action yet because of the threat of a lawsuit, which would probably allege violation of Harding's constitutional right to due process.

The skiers, skaters, bobsledders and hockey players flew to Norway. Harding stayed in Oregon until the last minute, waiting to see what would happen—both in the courts and among Olympic officials.

Before joining an Olympic team, every U.S. athlete must sign a code of conduct. They pledge to act "in such a manner that you bring credit and honor to yourself, your teammates, your national governing body, the USOC and the United States of America."

One of the problems with the rules, however well intentioned, was that the attack on Kerrigan occurred before either skater was officially a member of the Olympic team. That meant that, even when it was following parts of the Amateur Sports Act, the law that governs Olympic sports in the United States, the USOC might be violating others.

With most of the Olympic team in Lillehammer, the figure skating federation finally acted. It held a hearing and concluded that Harding had concealed knowledge of the crime. By then, it was up to the USOC to take disciplinary measures. It said it would hold its own inquiry in Oslo, and perhaps call Gillooley to testify.

And that's when Harding filed suit. She charged the USOC with violating her rights and asked for $25 million in damages.

The USOC, for all its anger, backed down. It won agreement that Harding would drop her suit if she was allowed to skate. The threat of the suit—and lawyers agreed Harding had a good chance of winning—had done the trick.

Harding flew to Lillehammer, where, she said, she was going to win a gold medal "and hang it on my wall forever." And she was cashing in already, signing a six-figure deal for exclusive interviews with a tabloid TV show.

The circus grew and grew. Kerrigan and Harding both moved into the Olympic Village and bumped into each other one day, exchanging a few pleasant words and then moving on. They practiced on the same ice rink, before hundred of reporters who normally wouldn't attend such sessions. Harding's e-mail account in the Olympic computer was accessed by reporters. She and Kerrigan were followed everywhere. Their dresses ... their hairstyles

ABOVE: Tonya Harding and
Nancy Kerrigan (foreground)
pass one another during
practice in Hamar, Norway.

ABOVE: Tonya Harding tries to compose herself after a late start to her free skating program at the 1994 Olympics. Moments later, she interrupted her program because of problems with her skates.

RIGHT: Nancy Kerrigan, winner of the silver medal at Lillehammer, performs her free skate program.

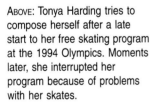

... oh, yes, their skating ... was analyzed down to the final inch.

Then they skated. And neither of them won.

Kerrigan took the silver medal again, behind 16-year-old Oksana Baiul of Ukraine. Harding, her drama running overtime, barely made it onto the ice and then had to tearfully ask judges for a restart after a lace on her gold-bladed skating boot broke. She finished eighth.

TV ratings were sky high, with almost half the number of Americans watching television tuned to the drama in Lillehammer.

Kerrigan took her silver medal to Disney World, where she rode with Mickey Mouse in the Main Street parade. Harding went back to Oregon and was arrested.

ABOVE: Ukraine's Oksana Baiul ends her performance in the technical program at Hamar Olympic Amphitheatre in Hamar, Norway.

RIGHT: Katarina Witt skates to *Carmen* during her freestyle presentation in the figure skating competition in Calgary in 1988. She won the gold.

LEFT: Oksana Baiul of Ukraine performs her free skating program at the 1994 Olympics, where she won the gold.

ABOVE: Ukrainian figure skater Oksana Baiul wipes away a tear after accepting her gold medal for figure skating at the Winter Olympics in 1994.

At first continuing to deny involvement, Harding won a stay of figure skating hearings so she could prepare for the world championships. But a week later, she pleaded guilty to conspiring to hinder the prosecution. She was given three years' probation, fined $160,000, ordered to do 500 hours of community service, forced to resign from the figure skating federation and undergo psychiatric counseling.

The federation later stripped her of her national title.

Eckhardt, Smith and Stant all were sentenced to 18 months in jail after copping pleas. Gillooley was sentenced to two years and fined $100,000 by Multnomah County Circuit Judge Donald Londer, who said the case had left an indelible stain on their city and the Olympic rings.

"All that will be recalled," Londer said, "is a band of thugs from Portland, Oregon, tried to rig the national figure skating association championships and the Olympics by stealth and violence."

It wasn't all a sordid scene in Lillehammer. In fact, the image that endures was soft as a baby's cheek and swaddled in red, white and blue.

Dan Jansen was the world's best short-distance speedskater. He had world records, world championships, a worldwide following—everything except an Olympic gold medal. His failures were among the most watched and most bewildering in the history of the Games.

Favored to win two gold medals in 1988, Jansen awoke the morning of his first race to hear the news that his sister, Jane Beres, had died of leukemia. He went to the oval in Calgary that night determined to win a gold for Jane in the 500 meters—but fell late in the race. The same thing happened in the 1,000—a gold medal within his reach, gravity took over and Jansen was flat on the ice.

Four years later, on an outdoor oval in Albertville, France, Jansen was done in again. He didn't fall, but he didn't win, victimized this time by faster skaters and soft ice that made his blades sink into the slush.

Like Harding and Kerrigan, Lillehammer gave Jansen an unexpected—and final—chance at that gold medal for Jane. And through the first two races at the spectacular Viking Ship skating hall in Hamar, it appeared that '94 would end just like '88 and '92.

Still the fastest man on ice, Jansen slipped in the 500 and failed to medal. His last shot was the 1,000, no longer one of his strongest distances. Or so he and most of the world thought.

With the Norwegian crowd cheering him on, Jansen started strongly in the 1,000, zipping through lap after lap at first-place pace. Then late in the race, on the far turn, Jansen faltered just a tad. His skate slipped. His right hand touched the ice. He kept going, righted himself and powered through the final strides to a world-record 1-minute, 12.43-seconds.

On the victory stand, Jansen accepted his long-sought gold medal with tears in his eyes. He sang along to the national anthem, and gave a little salute to his departed sister as the flag was raised. Then he took a victory lap with his infant daughter Jane—named after his sister—in his arms.

"My life," Jansen said, "is only different in the sense that I feel there is a weight off my shoulders. I feel like a new person."

ABOVE: Dan Jansen reacts after finishing with a world record time and a gold medal in the 1,000-meter race at the 1994 Winter Olympics.

OPPOSITE PAGE: Dan Jansen takes a victory lap with his baby daughter after the 1,000-meter event.

LEFT: Norwegian speedskater Johann Olav on his way to a world record time and a gold medal in the 10,000-meter event.

BELOW: Bonnie Blair wins her fourth career gold medal with this win in the 500-meter freestyle speedskating even in Hamar, Norway.

LEFT: Bonnie Blair celebrates her gold medal after winning her 1,000-meter race in Hamar, Norway.

BELOW: Bonnie Blair takes her victory lap with the Olympic mascots after winning her fifth gold medal.

LEFT: Picabo Street of the United States reacts in the finish area after completing her third training run in the downhill skiing event in 1994.

BELOW: American Tommy Moe leans through a turn in the downhill section of the combined alpine event in Norway in 1994.

Atlanta 1996

ABOVE: The logo for the 1996 Olympic Games, a torch and flame against a background of Georgia green.

BELOW: Atlanta, host city for the 1996 centennial Olympic Games.

CHAPTER XVI

Atlanta's Olympic Look

Each time an Olympics is held, it brings along its own look. Tokyo and Seoul offered the curving grace

ABOVE: President Juan Antonio Samaranch of the International Olympic Committee announces Atlanta as the winner in efforts to host the 1996 Olympic Games.

up what it had and come up with what it had not, all in modestly modern designs that will last long after the Games are over.

Just north of downtown, on the fringe of the Georgia Tech campus, new dormitories will house the athletes in apartments that are cozy but comfortable. There's a new swimming and diving complex there, too, and all of this will become part of the campus community once the Olympics are finished.

To the south of the city is the main Olympic stadium. Brick-clad and positioned just across a parking lot from Atlanta-Fulton County Stadium, the longtime home of baseball's Atlanta Braves, it will seat 80,000 fans for the Olympics, then be pared down to a 50,000-seat baseball field after the flame is extinguished. Fulton County Stadium will be demolished.

The main stadium, with a steel tower next door holding the Olympic flame, will be the scene of track and field and the opening and closing ceremonies. Those ceremonies are the toughest ticket at the Games, with best seats carrying a list price of $600, and the Atlanta organizers want the official start to be something that will leave spectators with ideas of both where they are and what to expect.

"The South is rich and diverse, and the ceremonies will be a vivid display of that great diversity," Payne said. The region has produced leaders such as Dr. Martin Luther King Jr. and President Jimmy Carter. It's come back time and time again from adversity. It is recognized as one of the best places in the United States to live and raise a family. It's not called "Hotlanta" for nothing.

But it's also a region that fostered slavery and human rights repression. The Ku Klux Klan burned crosses here long before anyone thought of lighting the Olympic flame. For every image of Tara, there's the reality of Techwood, one of the earliest and most forlorn of the nation's public housing projects—and a neighbor of several Olympic sites.

of the East. Moscow had the rugged look of socialism. Los Angeles was breezy and laid back.

Atlanta will be different from all the others. But just how will that difference be felt?

The American South will be a focus of the Atlanta Games, chief organizer Billy Payne promised almost from the beginning. That means a look of bustling business, gleaming steel and fast-track technology.

But there's a human side, too, that Payne and his cohorts want to present. It was that human side that got the Georgia capital the Games in the first place, and it will be on prominent display during the summer of '96.

Payne likes to describe his Games as "the biggest peacetime event mankind has ever staged." To that end, Atlanta has spruced

While it wants to emphasize what is right with its city, Atlanta has no plans to whitewash what is wrong.

"We are who we are, and we're very proud of that," Payne said. "This will be a statement of who we are."

To help get that statement across, ACOG hired Emmy-winning TV producer Don Mischer to put the ceremonies together. "Recent history has proven to us all that the success of the Games, the mood that will be set, can be made most clear through the achievement of a successful opening ceremony," Payne said. "It is the first and best opportunity to communicate vividly that passion that our community feels for the Olympic movement."

For the first time, the opening ceremonies July 19 will be staged on a day to themselves. Atlanta added a 17th day to its Olympic calendar, giving NBC a prime-time Friday night special and the Games another opportunity to showcase what's ahead. Some 3.5 billion people worldwide will watch the 10,000 athletes parade into the stadium—they will march from Fulton County Stadium, because there's no room for them to sit in the sold-out main arena—and see Atlanta unveil its latest image: Olympic host.

"It's something you can't take lightly," Mischer said.

To make sure he captured the flavor for the town, Mischer spent months talking with its people, from government leaders to business executives to community activists. The winner of more than a dozen Emmy awards for prime-time spectacles and the producer of such celebrations as the opening of EuroDisney and the 100th

BELOW: The Olympic Stadium is the site of opening and closing ceremonies as well as athletic competition. After the Games, it will be converted to a baseball park for the Atlanta Braves.

birthday of the Statue of Liberty, Mischer said the Olympics would be something special.

"It is on a grander scale than anything," he said.

So here we are, almost 10 years from Payne's Olympic dream and ready to open the Games. What will it be like? Let's take a look at a typical day for an Olympic tourist in Atlanta:

The "Smiths" are fans—no, make that sports nuts. Bob and Debbie jog and play golf. The kids, Jeff and Jennifer, are involved in afterschool basketball, gymnastics, soccer and bowling. Free time is spent rooting for the local teams—the baseball Braves, the football Falcons, the basketball Hawks and the hockey Knights. Bob and Debbie went to the University of Georgia, Billy Payne's alma mater, so there's Bulldog fever in the house, too.

From their home in suburban Conyers, the Smiths can almost see the Olympic flame. What better way to spend a long weekend in the summer of 1996 than watching all they can of the Olympics right there in their hometown?

The Smiths have budgeted $1,200 to carry them through three days of Olympic tickets. That's just over $400 a day, and a family of four who want to see a lot of sports can expect to spend that easily, even before they've bought a souvenir or chugged down a soda.

For the Smiths, the Olympic adventure starts on Friday, July 26.

AN EARLY START

Summer in Georgia is in full swing as the day begins. The morning dawns clear and dewy, with a forecast of afternoon highs in the low 90s and humidity to match. No wonder the Olympic organizers decided to stage equestrian events just past sunrise, and that's where we find the Smith family shortly after 7 a.m.

The equestrian events are staged at Georgia International Horse Park, in the Smiths' hometown east of the city. It's an easy commute for the Smiths, although—

with restrictions on private cars throughout the Olympic region—they arrived here by bus, leaving the family van with the "How 'Bout Them Dogs!" bumper sticker in a park-and-ride not far from home. They'll take Olympic buses and MARTA rapid-rail throughout their visit to the Games.

To watch the riders and horses gallop through the Georgia clay, the Smiths paid $11 apiece. These tickets were among the easiest to come by, with Bob popping into an ACOG ticket kiosk just a couple of days before and taking his pick. But soon, the family will be sitting in seats they were truly fortunate to reach.

ON YOUR MARK, GET SET ...

Tickets for track and field events are among the toughest to get in Atlanta. Most of the seats go to corporate sponsors or other well-connected folks. Season-ticket holders for the Braves had a chance to get preferred seats for track prelims, the morning events that usually consist of heats and a few finals. The Smiths didn't have any of those VIP links, but they were lucky enough to come up with four seats for the opening morning of track through the public ticket sale that began in May 1995. They sent in their order, waiting several months before learning the good news. Now they are sitting in the new Olympic stadium, the sun rising and warming the cheap seats that cost $22 each. That's not bad to watch the start of the decathlon, some heats in the men's and women's 100 meters and the end of one of the glamour events, the women's marathon. Unlike the men's race that will end the Games on Aug. 9, the women's marathon started in the cool of the morning and will be over before Atlanta really bakes.

The Smiths could spend most of the day at track, before the stadium is cleared for the night session. But it's getting hot, and there's a lot more to see. Thankfully, the next stop is indoors.

PUT SOME MUSCLE INTO IT

Hopping on a MARTA train, the Smiths soon are in the middle of Olympic Atlanta.

With a change of trains at Five Points, they debark at the Georgia World Congress Center, a sprawling complex of exhibition halls and meeting rooms that is host to six Olympic events. Today's stop is weightlifting, a fairly easy ticket at $20 each. If they chose to, the Smiths could stop in next door for the first day of team handball or a couple of judo matches; seats are available on a walkup basis. But they will be back at the Congress Center on Saturday July 27 for table tennis and again Monday, July 29, for fencing.

The next stop is just a short walk away. And, like the morning's track, it's a tough ticket that the Smiths clutch as they make there way across a pedestrian plaza to the Georgia Dome.

HOOP TIME

The Georgia Dome looks like a big, white circus tent from the outside. Inside, it's a two-ring Olympic circus with a couple of the biggest draws of the Games.

Our intrepid family of fans is here for hoops—and American hoops, at that. The U.S. team of NBA stars is playing in a late-afternoon game before a sellout crowd of more than 30,000. That's about half the Dome's capacity, and that's because the building also is used for gymnastics, which also sells out its seats. While the Smiths were lucky enough to get their basketball wishes fulfilled in the general sale, at $16 each, they couldn't get their hands on any gymnastics tickets. Oh well, some things you just have to watch on TV.

The Smiths may leave the Dome before the final buzzer to grab some dinner and mingle in one Olympic venue where admission doesn't cost a cent.

A STROLL THROUGH THE PLAZA

When Atlanta's Olympic planners went to Barcelona for the 1992 Games, they were struck by the massive crowds that gathered each night in streets and plazas outside the stadiums. Most of the people there didn't have tickets, and might not even have been sports fans. But they were there to enjoy the ambience in the open air.

Atlanta is a closed-up city. You rarely see people on the street in midday, especially in mid-summer when everyone seeks air conditioning. And there were no areas even resembling a public park or piazza where people could hang out and soak up some Olympic atmosphere.

Thus was born Centennial Olympic Park, a 60-acre oasis amid the glass towers and concrete parking garages of downtown. And on this hot summer evening, it's packed with folks who come to see what all the fuss is about.

As they stroll the plaza, the Smiths search for their bricks—among hundreds of thousands purchased for $35 each and engraved with the name of the buyer, then used to pave the plaza. As they wander, there are snacks to munch, souvenirs to check out and pins to be bartered. It's a good place to spend some time away from the Olympics and yet feel part of the Games, too.

Soon, the rest is over. Their bricks tracked down, their stomachs full and their wallets a little lighter, the Smiths head for their final stop of a long day at the Games.

SPLASHING TO A SCORE

A shuttle bus takes the Smith family to Georgia Tech, and the Olympic Aquatic Center. The big complex of pools is the place for swimming, synchronized swimming and diving. The night of July 26, however, it's water polo on the schedule. The Smiths were able to buy tickets in the general mail-order sale for $32 each, although there were seats available just before the game started.

ABOVE: The Georgia Tech Aquatic Center, on the campus of the Georgia Institute of Technology.

The Smiths stay until the end, then it's onto another shuttle bus and a 15-minute ride to the parking lot, where they left their van. It's nearly 11 p.m., more than 17 hours since they left home, and less than eight hours before they leave for Saturday's morning session of Olympic tennis at Stone Mountain, about 16 miles east of the city.

Nobody said it was easy being an Olympic fan.

But there's a lot more to Atlanta than the Olympic Games—and more than just CNN and a bunch of Rhett and Scarlett leftovers.

So, pass the peanuts, and let's look at what else we can expect from the Summer Games in the Deep South.

CAN YOU PLEASE TURN UP THE AIR CONDITIONING?

First of all, remember: This IS the Deep South. That's Deep, as in Deep Fried. There will be no wind-chill readings when the Games open July 19. The National Weather Service says the average high temperature for Atlanta in late July and early August is 88 degrees. And this ain't no dry heat. The humidity that floods up from the Gulf of Mexico can sap the strongest athlete or spectator. Distance runners will be especially affected, including those in the final event, the men's marathon, which starts in mid-afternoon.

We should get an idea of how the weather conditions will affect Olympic athletes from results of a series of test events, which began back in the fall of 1994. And the U.S. Olympic track team will be well-acclimated after an international meet

Pinheads of the World, Unite!

They can be as big as the bottom of a coffee mug or as small as a fingernail. They come painted, gilded, lacquered and buffed. Gold, silver and bronze.

They are Olympic pins, and they are coins of the realm at the Games.

These pins have been around since the first modern Games in 1896. Originally, they were to identify athletes, officials and journalists, a quasi-credential system. But by the Stockholm Games in 1912, athletes were trading pins as goodwill gestures with other competitors. Soon, fans got into the act. And by 1980, pin trading had become an unofficial Olympic sport, with all big sponsors, most teams and a large percentage of media outlets and other related business producing special pins for the Games.

"Pinheads," as the traders call themselves, stake out their turf from the airport to the gate of the Olympic Village, displaying pins on hats, scarfs, T-shirts and rugs. Although some companies sell their pins, most of the market is barter. Coca-Cola Co., which produces some of the most popular Olympic pins, estimated that some 600,000 pins of all types exchanged hands at its pin-trading center in the Lillehammer Winter Games in 1994, and you can bet there were at least than many swapped on the streets and in restaurants, bars and hotel lobbies.

Atlanta should see millions of pins traded.

at the Olympic Stadium May 3-5, 1996, and the U.S. track team trials there June 14-23.

I'LL TAKE A SIDE ORDER OF GRITS PARMIGIANA

Southern cooking is different. First of all, there's no such thing as "Southern Lite." Lots of butter on the biscuits and lots of gravy on the pork, chicken and greens—that's the way Atlantans like it. Fried catfish is a local specialty, and very tasty. So is the barbecue, usually pork or chicken. Ribs are excellent. It all goes well with hush puppies, little balls or tubes of corn meal that are deep fried. And of course, there's grits.

This looks like oatmeal, and it's often eaten at breakfast. But grits come from hominy, a coarse grain. They are mashed down and boiled into a sticky paste and served very hot. You'll find them on menus at any time of the day or night as a substitute for cereal or potatoes. Try them plain, with butter and salt, or topped with maple syrup. But, no, Italian restaurants in

New Arrivals

Atlanta will have more events in more sports than any Olympics before. Some of the new additions:

Mountain Biking. In the race to attract younger audiences, the IOC added this staple of Saturday teen-age fun. Venue: Georgia International Horse Park.

Beach Volleyball. A TV favorite, beach volleyball for men and women will take place far from a beach, on an artificial field of sand just outside Atlanta.

Women's Softball. Part of the IOC's efforts to bring more women into the Games, softball will make its debut in the western Georgia city of Columbus. The United States is a favorite for the gold medal.

Atlanta won't offer grits with tomato sauce and cheese.

Atlanta is not all Southern fried. It's a cosmopolitan city with great food of any kind—Chinese, Italian, French, Indian, whatever your taste. Chops is generally rated as one of the best steak houses in America. And for a local treat on a budget, don't miss the Varsity Drive-In. It's located just north of downtown, not far from many of the main venues. The hot dogs are among the best in the world.

Of course, Atlanta has plenty of fast food. In fact, McDonald's is a corporate sponsor of the Atlanta Games and has even propped up the Golden Arches inside the Olympic village, the first time Olympic athletes can enjoy fast food right in their own secure compound.

LAST TRAIN TO HARTSFIELD

The joke among air travelers in the eastern half of the United States is that when they die, whether they head toward heaven or hell, they'll have to change planes in Atlanta.

Well, Hartsfield International Airport is pretty busy, and mighty big.

It covers 2.2 million square feet south of Atlanta, making it the biggest passenger terminal in the world. Every year, 45 million people pass through Hartsfield, catching more scheduled flights than at any of the world's other airports—2,000 a day. And for the Olympics, it has added a new international terminal that dwarfs full airports in most other cities.

For all its size, taming Hartsfield is fairly easy. When you get off the plane, head for the shuttle train that runs from each arrivals wing to the baggage claim and transit center. The shuttle is clean and quick. The only drawback may be the computer generated voice—known locally as Hal, after the robot in *2001: A Space Odyssey*—that warns to watch out for the closing doors. Try not to laugh when you hear it, and do step back.

There are plenty of ways to get from the airport to downtown. If you're traveling light, take MARTA—that's Metropolitan Atlanta Rapid Transit Authority, which runs a light-rail system that cris-crosses near Peachtree Street and the Georgia Dome. It takes about 20 minutes and costs $1.25. The trains are clean and safe. In fact, the head of the IOC evaluation commission, Gunnar Ericsson of Sweden, and his son rode MARTA to the airport after their inquiry visit in 1990. They were very impressed—the train they rode was as clean and well patrolled as the one they took as part of their official tour the previous day.

Other Mascots

Izzy is the latest in a long and venerated line of Olympic mascots. A few other notables have included:

SCHUSS. The grandfather of all Olympic mascots, this beast on skis appeared at the 1968 Winter Games in Grenoble, France. He had a bulky white head and a body in red and blue, the tri-colors of the French Flag. "It wasn't a person, and it wasn't an animal," said Michele Verdier, the IOC director of special projects, who was a Grenoble schoolgirl at the time. "You could say it was the original 'Whatizit.'"

MISHA. A roly-poly bear, this was the mascot of the Moscow Games in 1980. Misha was popular with Soviet children and, because of the U.S.-led boycott of the Moscow Olympics, souvenirs bearing Misha's likeness have jumped in value.

VUCKO. A mountain wolf with a knowing leer, this was the mascot of the 1984 Winter Games in Sarajevo. When organizers wanted to introduce their symbol at a news conference in New York, they led a real wolf on a chain into the room. The audience gasped and scattered quickly.

SAM. Only Walt Disney could have come up with this one. Sam the Eagle wore a big bowtie, a friendly smile and a red-white-and-blue striped top hat as mascot of the '84 Games in Los Angeles.

HOWDY & HIDY. The first dual mascots, these polar bears in red bandannas and cowboy hats saturated the Calgary Winter Games in 1988. They were everywhere, posing for pictures, waving to fans and appearing on everything from T-shirts to key rings. "We all know what Hidy does," one reporter wrote, "but what is Howdy's duty?"

HODORI. A jaunty tiger was the Seoul mascot in 1988. Hodori stood on his hind legs, usually wearing a black Korean bowler with a festival ribbon streaming from the top. He was a marketing success.

MAGIQUE. This was a second-generation mascot of the 1992 Winter Games in Albertville. The organizers originally wanted a chamois, a small mountain goat, but the symbol never caught on. Magique was a late replacement, a mountain fairy in the shape of a star with a red pointed hat on its blue body. Magique was unique.

COBI. The smiling, straight-backed mascot of the 1992 Games in Barcelona, this was one weird dog. Cobi was laughed at when organizers unveiled the idea but quickly caught on and became a very successful symbol of the Barcelona Games. The artist who created Cobi said he first drew the dog when he was stoned on marijuana.

HAAKON & KRISTIN. For the first time, Olympic organizers considered actual people worthy of being corporate symbols. The mascots of the 1994 Winter Games in Lillehammer were based on Prince Haakon, a medieval leader of Norway who was rescued as a child by skiing soldiers, and his Aunt Kristin, who helped to hide him out during the war.

It's a Money-Making Mascot

Of all the things that Billy Payne did to bring the Olympics to Atlanta and then go about making sure that everything was ready, the one that brought perhaps the biggest howls of protest was the choice of the mascot.

Since Grenoble, France, used a skiing beast named Schuss as its symbol at the Winter Games in 1968, the Olympics have been awash in mascots—from beavers (Lake Placid 1980) to eagles (Los Angeles 1984) to cuddly bears (Calgary 1988) to kids (Lillehammer 1994).

Usually, they are animals. Kristin and Haakon, the mascots of the Lillehammer Winter Games, were the first people used, and they were at first represented as cartoons. The Albertville Winter Games in 1992 featured Magique, a full-figured mountain sprite who was part person, part star.

But Atlanta's choice was totally different. Even its name was out of the ordinary.

And for a long time, the world wasn't quiet sure what to make of Whatizit.

The Atlanta mascot is a first-of-its-kind, computer-generated ... er ....thing. It's blue with white teeth, red sneakers, lightning bolts for eyebrows and the Olympic rings spread on its head and tail. It was unveiled from a cloak of secrecy during the closing ceremonies of the 1992 Games in Barcelona, and almost immediately people started asking the Atlanta organizers to explain it.

The concept was clever. Whatizit could be anything—or nothing. In computer language, it could "morph" into just about whatever might be connected with the Olympics—"Itzaboxer" sported boxing gloves and helmet; "Itzarunner" showed up with spiked shoes and singlet; "Itzafan" lined up for tickets; and so on.

But its shape—described as everything

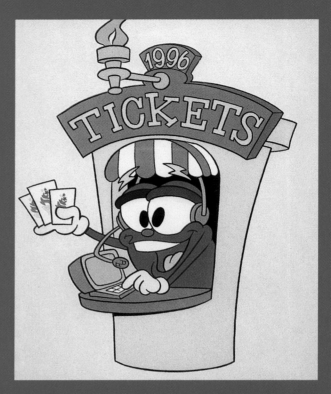

from a blue tadpole to a sperm—and the newness of the whole thing brought instant ridicule.

"It's a bad marriage of the Pillsbury Doughboy and the ugliest California Raisin," said Matt Groening, creator of "The Simpsons," who's drawn some pretty weird characters himself.

Payne wasn't worried. "We are going to get the last laugh with Whatizit," he said. "I guarantee it."

ACOG had prepared a very colorful videotape, featuring Payne and a bunch of computer screens, that clearly and concisely explained the concept behind Whatizit. But for some reason, it decided against showing the tape to the international news media gathered in Barcelona. That left journalists to draw their own conclusions and even ask IOC President Juan Antonio Samaranch what he thought. Samaranch, a firm believer that there is no such thing as bad publicity, played along.

"I like this mascot," he told a news conference the day after the Barcelona Games ended. "It's name is Whatizit, and I like it. But this does not mean the mascot cannot change."

Sure enough, the mascot has changed. And so have people's views of it, as far as being a successful symbol. Adults might have gawked at Whatizit and backed away. But Payne knew his market—kids. They embraced the blue blob, snapping up anything with Whatizit's image, from T-shirts to mugs to posters to stuffed, plush Whatizit toys.

In 1993, about a year after the creature sprang to life, ACOG went to schools and surveyed children on what changes they would make to the mascot. They also were asked, "How about a name?"

Back came the responses: Bulk him up. So Whatizit started popping muscles from his shoulders and arms. The big teeth disappeared and a more human-like mouth took over. And to top it off, Whatizit became "Izzy."

By whatever name, the morph has proven Payne to be correct. ACOG is flooded with hundreds of requests for personal appearances for people dressed in Izzy costumes. Children across the country have sent in more than 100,000 stories about Izzy. And marketing—the bottom line for any mascot—has been an absolute smash. ACOG projects sales of

Izzy merchandise to top off at $25 million-$30 million. What's more, Izzy is ready to become a TV star. An animated cartoon series was planned for late 1995 and '96, with a girlfriend for Izzy among the cast.

Itzasuccess.

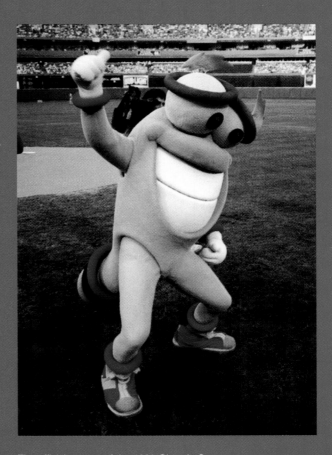

The official mascot of the 1996 Olympic Games.

Atlanta Adds Up

A look at Atlanta and its Olympic Games, by the numbers:

1—million. The additional number of people who have visited Atlanta each year since the IOC awarded the 1996 Games to the city.

1.6—billion dollars. The budget of the organizing committee, the Atlanta Committee for the Olympic Games. It's expected to produce a surplus—or "contingency fund"—of $60 million.

2.8—million people, the population of the Atlanta metropolitan area.

3—number of U.S. cities that have previously hosted Olympics. Los Angeles (1932, 1984) and St. Louis (1904) hosted the Summer Olympics and Lake Placid (1932, 1980) was the site of the Winter Olympics.

5.1—billion dollars, the expected impact of the Games on the economy of Georgia.

7.5—million, the number of tickets to be sold for the Games, a record.

21—venues for Olympic sports, from Savannah (yachting) on Georgia's Atlantic Coast to the Ocoee River (white-water canoeing) on the Georgia-Tennessee border.

25—dollars. Average ticket price.

34—streets in Atlanta with Peachtree in their name.

51—votes from IOC members awarded the Centennial Games to Atlanta on September 18, 1990.

62—percent of Atlanta residents questioned in a September 1993 Atlanta *Journal-Constitution* poll who believe the Olympics are so important they will determine how the world views their city in the future.

73—stories in the Westin Peachtree Plaza, the tallest hotel in the Western Hemisphere.

80—percent of the U.S. population who live within a two-hour flight of Atlanta.

88—degrees, the average high temperatures for Atlanta during the Olympic period of late July and early August.

100—years since the first modern Olympics, in Athens in 1896.

200—dollars a day, what an average visitor spends during a business trip to Atlanta. That includes hotel, meals and entertainment.

404—area code for the Atlanta region. It covers 3,300 square miles—the world's largest toll-free telephone calling zone.

451—million dollars, the record price NBC paid for U.S. television rights to the Atlanta Olympics.

2,000—flights a day in and out of Hartsfield International Airport, the world's largest.

15,500—athletes, coaches and officials expected to be housed in the Olympic Village.

54,615—hotel rooms in the metro Atlanta area.

85,000—seats in the main Olympic Stadium, site of the opening and closing ceremonies and track and field events.

600,000—fans, the peak daily attendance anticipated for the Games, on Day 11 of competition July 31.

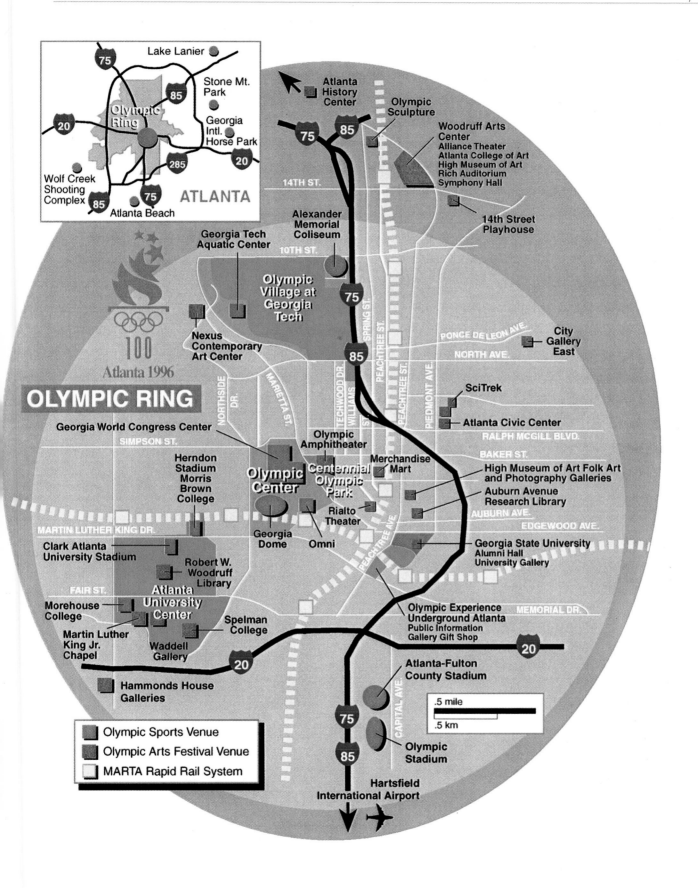

OLYMPIC RING

Atlanta 1996

Inset map: ATLANTA

- 75 Lake Lanier
- 85 Stone Mt. Park
- Olympic Ring
- 20
- Georgia Intl. Horse Park
- 285
- 20
- 75
- 85
- Wolf Creek Shooting Complex
- Atlanta Beach

Map labels:
- Atlanta History Center
- Olympic Sculpture
- Woodruff Arts Center / Alliance Theater / Atlanta College of Art / High Museum of Art / Rich Auditorium / Symphony Hall
- 14th Street Playhouse
- 14TH ST.
- Alexander Memorial Coliseum
- Georgia Tech Aquatic Center
- 10TH ST.
- Olympic Village at Georgia Tech
- 75
- SPRING ST.
- PEACHTREE ST.
- PONCE DE LEON AVE.
- City Gallery East
- NORTH AVE.
- 85
- Nexus Contemporary Art Center
- NORTHSIDE DR.
- MARIETTA ST.
- TECHWOOD DR.
- WILLIAMS ST.
- PEACHTREE ST.
- PIEDMONT AVE.
- SciTrek
- Atlanta Civic Center
- Georgia World Congress Center
- SIMPSON ST.
- Olympic Amphitheater
- RALPH MCGILL BLVD.
- BAKER ST.
- Herndon Stadium Morris Brown College
- Olympic Center
- Centennial Olympic Park
- Merchandise Mart
- High Museum of Art Folk Art and Photography Galleries
- Auburn Avenue Research Library
- AUBURN AVE.
- MARTIN LUTHER KING DR.
- Georgia Dome
- Rialto Theater
- Omni
- PEACHTREE AVE.
- EDGEWOOD AVE.
- Clark Atlanta University Stadium
- Robert W. Woodruff Library
- Georgia State University Alumni Hall University Gallery
- FAIR ST.
- Atlanta University Center
- Morehouse College
- Spelman College
- Martin Luther King Jr. Chapel
- Waddell Gallery
- Olympic Experience Underground Atlanta Public Information Gallery Gift Shop
- MEMORIAL DR.
- 20
- Hammonds House Galleries
- 20
- Atlanta-Fulton County Stadium
- CAPITAL AVE.
- 75
- Olympic Stadium
- 85
- Hartsfield International Airport

Scale: .5 mile / .5 km

Legend:
- ■ Olympic Sports Venue
- ■ Olympic Arts Festival Venue
- □ MARTA Rapid Rail System

SCHEDULE OF OLYMPICS EVENTS

The competition schedule for the 1996 Olympics, with sport, venue, date, type of competition, starting time and range of ticket prices (all times EDT):

Opening Ceremony
Olympic Stadium
Tickets $212-$637

July 19 8:30 p.m.

Archery
Stone Mountain, Ga.
Tickets $11-$27

July 29 Women's preliminaries 9 a.m.
July 30 Men's preliminaries 9 a.m.
July 31 Women's preliminaries 9 a.m., finals 2 p.m.
Aug. 1 Men's preliminaries 9 a.m., finals 2 p.m.
Aug. 2 Women's and men's team finals, quarterfinals, semifinals 9 a.m.; women's and men's team finals 1:30 p.m.

Track and Field
Olympic Stadium
Tickets $22-$265

July 26 Men's 20-kilometer walk final; men's shot put, women's 100-meters, men's 100-meters, women's 800-meters, preliminaries, 8 a.m. Men's shot put final; women's javelin, women's 100, men's high jump, men's 100, men's 800, women's 5,000, men's 10,000, preliminaries, 6 p.m.

July 27 Women's heptathlon 100-meter hurdles, women's triple jump, men's 400 meters, women's heptathlon high jump, women's 400 meters, men's hammer throw, preliminaries, 9:15 a.m. Women's javelin final; women's 100 semifinals and final; men's 100 semifinals and final; women's 800 semifinals; women's heptathlon shot put, men's triple jump, men's 800, women's heptathlon 200, women's 10,000, preliminaries, 5:30 p.m.

July 28 Women's marathon final; women's heptathlon long jump, women's discus, men's 110-meter hurdles, women's 400-meter hurdles, preliminaries, 7:30 a.m. Men's hammer throw, men's high jump, men's triple jump, women's 5,000, women's heptathlon javelin and heptathlon 800, finals; men's 800 semifinals; men's 110 hurdles, men's 400, women's 400, 3:30 p.m.

July 29 Women's 10-kilometer walk, final; men's discus, men's 200 meters, women's 200 meters, men's 1,500 meters, men's 400-meter hurdles, preliminaries. Men's discus, men's triple jump, women's 800, men's 10,000, finals; men's 110 hurdles, semifinals and final; women's 400, semifinals; men's 400, semifinals; women's 400 hurdles semifinals; men's 200, women's 200, men's 3,000 steeple-chase, preliminaries, 6 p.m.

July 31 Men's decathlon 100 meters, men's pole vault, women's 1,500 meters, men's decathlon long jump, women's 100-meter hurdles, men's decathlon shot put, preliminaries, 9 p.m. Men's discus, women's 400 hurdles, men's 400, women's 400, men's 800, finals; men's decathlon 400, men's 5,000, preliminaries, 5:15 p.m.

Aug. 1 Women's wheelchair 800 meters, men's wheelchair 1,500 meters, finals; men's decathlon 110-meter hurdles, women's high jump, men's decathlon discus, women's long jump, preliminaries, 8 a.m. Men's long jump, men's 400 hurdles, women's 200, men's 200, men's decathlon pole vault, decathlon javelin, decathlon 1,500, finals; women's 100 hurdles semifinals and final; women's 1,500, men's 1,500, semifinals; men's 5,000 semifinals, 2 p.m.

Aug. 2 Men's 50-kilometer walk, final; men's javelin, men's 400-meter relay, women's 400-meter relay, men's 1,600-meter relay, preliminaries, 7:30 a.m. Men's pole vault, women's shot put, women's long jump, men's 3,000 steeple-chase, women's 10,000, finals; women's 400 relay, men's 400 relay, men's 1,600 relay, semifinals; women's 1,600 relay, preliminaries, 6 p.m.

Aug. 3 Women's high jump, men's javelin, women's 400-meter relay, men's 400-meter relay, women's 1,500 meters, men's 1,500 meters, men's 5,000 meters, women's 1,600-meter relay, men's 1,600-meter relay, finals, 6:30 p.m.

Aug. 4 Men's marathon, final, 6:30 p.m.

Badminton
Georgia State University, Atlanta
Tickets $16-$38

July 24 Women's and men's singles preliminaries 9 a.m.
July 25 Women's doubles, men's doubles, men's singles preliminaries 9 a.m.
July 26 Women's singles, men's singles, mixed doubles preliminaries 9 a.m.
July 27 Women's singles, men's and women's doubles, mixed doubles preliminaries 9 a.m.
July 28 Men's and women's doubles quarterfinals 9 a.m.
July 28 Women's and men's singles quarterfinals 8 p.m.
July 29 Mixed doubles quarterfinal, women's doubles semifinal 9 a.m.
July 30 Women's and men's singles semifinals, women's and men's doubles bronze medal 9 a.m.
July 31 Women's and men's doubles gold medal,

July 31 Women's and men's doubles gold medal, women's and men's singles bronze medal, mixed doubles bronze medal 9 a.m.
Aug. 1 Women's and men's singles gold medal, mixed doubles gold medal 9 a.m.

Baseball
Atlanta Fulton County Stadium
Tickets $7-$64
July 20 Preliminaries 10.a.m., 3 p.m., 8 p.m.
July 21 Preliminaries 3 p.m., 8 p.m.
July 22 Preliminaries 10 a.m., 3 p.m., 8 p.m.
July 23 Preliminaries 10 a.m., 3 p.m., 8 p.m.
July 24 Preliminaries 3 p.m., 8 p.m.
July 25 Preliminaries 10 a.m., 3 p.m., 8 p.m.
July 27 Preliminaries 10 a.m., 3 p.m., 8 p.m.
July 28 Preliminaries 10 a.m., 3 p.m., 8 p.m.
July 29 Preliminaries 10 a.m., 3 p.m., 8 p.m.
July 30 Preliminaries 10 a.m., 3 p.m., 8 p.m.
Aug. 1 Semifinals 2 p.m., 7 p.m.
Aug. 2 Bronze and gold medal games 2 p.m., 7 p.m.

Basketball
Atlanta University Center, Georgia Dome
Tickets $11-$265
July 20 Men's preliminaries 10 a.m., 3 p.m., 8 p.m.
July 21 Women's preliminaries 10 a.m., 3 p.m., 8 p.m.
July 22 Men's preliminaries 10 a.m., 3 p.m., 8 p.m.
July 23 Women's preliminaries 10 a.m., 3 p.m., 8 p.m.
July 24 Men's preliminaries 10 a.m., 3 p.m., 8 p.m.
July 25 Women's preliminaries 10 a.m., 3 p.m., 8 p.m.
July 26 Men's preliminaries 10 a.m., 3 p.m., 8 p.m.
July 27 Women's preliminaries 10 a.m., 3 p.m., 8 p.m.
July 28 Men's preliminaries 10 a.m., 5 p.m., 8 p.m.
July 29 Women's preliminaries 10 a.m., 3 p.m., 8 p.m.
July 30 Men's quarterfinals and classification 10 a.m., 3 p.m., 8 p.m.
July 31 Women's classification and quarterfinals 10 a.m., 3 p.m., 8 p.m.
Aug. 1 Men's and women's classification, men's semifinals 10 a.m., 3 p.m., 8 p.m.
Aug. 2 Men's classification, Women's semifinals, 10 a.m., 3 p.m., 8 p.m.
Aug. 3 Women's classification, men's bronze and gold medals 10 a.m., 3 p.m., 8 p.m.
Aug. 4 Women's bronze and gold medals 9:30 a.m.

Boxing
Georgia Tech
Tickets $27-$186
July 20 Preliminaries 1:30 p.m. and 8 p.m.
July 21 Preliminaries 1:30 p.m. and 8 p.m.
July 22 Preliminaries 1:30 p.m. and 8 p.m.
July 23 Preliminaries 1:30 p.m. and 8 p.m.
July 24 Preliminaries 1:30 p.m. and 8 p.m.
July 25 Preliminaries 1:30 p.m. and 8 p.m.
July 26 Preliminaries 1:30 p.m. and 8 p.m.

July 27 Preliminaries 1:30 p.m. and 8 p.m.
July 28 Preliminaries 1:30 p.m. and 8 p.m.
July 30 Quarterfinals 1:30 p.m. and 8 p.m.
July 31 Quarterfinals 1:30 p.m. and 8 p.m.
Aug. 1 Semifinals light flyweight, bantamweight, lightweight, middleweight, heavyweight, 8 p.m.
Aug. 2 Semifinals flyweight, featherweight, light welterweight, light middleweight, light heavyweight, super heavyweight, 8 p.m.
Aug. 3 Gold medals lightweight, light flyweight, bantamweight, lightweight, welterweight, middleweight, heavyweight, 1:30 p.m.
Aug. 4 Gold medals flyweight, featherweight, light welterweight, light middleweight, light heavyweight, super heavyweight, 1:30 p.m.

Canoe-kayak
Tickets $11-$32
Slalom
Ocoee River, Cleveland, Tenn.
July 26 Training runs 10 a.m.
July 27 Women's K-1 finals, men's C-1 finals 10 a.m.
July 29 Men's C-2 finals, men's K-1 finals 10 a.m.
Sprint
Lake Lanier, Gainesville, Ga.
July 30 Men's 1000 meter kayak and canoe, all classes; women's 500 meter K-4, preliminaries 9 a.m., repechage 2:30 p.m.
July 31 Men's 500 meter kayak and canoe, all classes; women's 500 meter K-1 and K-2, preliminaries 9 a.m., repechage 2:30 p.m.
Aug. 1 Men's 1000 meter kayak and canoe, all classes; women's 500 meter K-4, semifinals, 9 a.m.
Aug. 2 Men's 500 meter kayak and canoe, all classes; women's 500 meter K-1 and K-2, semifinals 9 a.m.
Aug. 3 Men's 1000 meter kayak and canoe, all classes; women's 500 meter K-4, finals 9 a.m.
Aug. 5 Men's 500 meter kayak and canoe, all classes; women's 500 meter K-1 and K-2, finals 9 a.m.

Cycling
Mountain Bike Racing
Georgia International Horse Park
Tickets $16
July 30 Women's and men's individual cross country 10 a.m.
Road Racing
Atlanta
Free
July 21 Women's road race 11 a.m.
July 31 Men's road race 8:30 a.m.
Aug. 3 Women's and men's individual time trial 8:30 a.m.

Track Racing

Stone Mountain Park
Tickets $27-$37

July 24 Men's individual pursuit qualifying and quarterfinal, women's and men's 200 meter sprint qualifying, men's 1 kilometer time trial final 10 a.m. aqnd 4:30 p.m.

July 25 Women's individual pursuit qualifying, men's individual pursuit semifinal, men's 200 meter sprint qualifying, women's sprint octos final, men's and women's sprint repechage, men's individual pursuit final 9 a.m.

July 26 Men's team pursuit qualifying, women's sprint quarterfinal TB, men's team pursuit quarterfinals, women's sprint semifinals and semifinal TB, women's individual pursuit quarterfinal, women's sprint 5-8 final 8:30 a.m.

July 27 Men's sprint quarterfinal, women's individual pursuit semifinal, men's team pursuit semifinal, men's and women's sprint final, men's spring quarterfinal TB, women's sprint final TB, men's sprint semifinal and semifinal TB, men's sprint 5-8 final, men's team pursuit final 11:15 a.m.

July 28 Women and men's points race final, men's sprint final, women's individual pursuit final 11:15 a.m.

Diving

Georgia Tech
Tickets $22-$159

July 26 Women's platform preliminaries 3 p.m.
July 27 Women's platform semifinal and final 11:30 a.m.
July 28 Men's springboard preliminaries 8 p.m.
July 29 Men's springboard semifinal and final 11:30 a.m.
July 30 Women's springboard preliminaries 8 p.m.
July 31 Women's springboard semifinal and final 11:30 a.m.
Aug. 1   Men's platform preliminaries 8 p.m.
Aug. 2   Men's platform semifinal and final 10 p.m.

Equestrian

Georgia International Horse Park
Tickets $11-$79
Dressage
July 27 Team preliminaries 8:30 a.m.
July 29 Team preliminaries and finals 8:30 a.m.
July 31 Individual 10 a.m.
Aug. 3   Individual freestyle final 9 a.m.
Jumping
July 29 Jumping qualifier 8:30 a.m.
Aug. 1   Team jumping preliminary and final 8:30 a.m.
Aug. 4   Individual jumping final 10 a.m.

Three Day
July 21 Team dressage preliminaries 9 a.m.
July 22 Team dressage preliminaries 9 a.m.
July 23 Team speed and endurance, individual dressage 7 a.m.
July 24 Team jumping and individual dressage 9 a.m.
July 25 Individual speed, endurance 7:30 a.m.
July 26 Individual jumping 11 a.m.

Fencing

Georgia World Congress Center
Tickets $11-$27

July 20 Men's individual epee, preliminaries, quarterfinals, semifinals, bronze and gold medals 10 a.m. and 3 p.m.

July 21 Women's individual epee preliminaries, quarterfinals, semifinals, bronze and gold medals 8 a.m. and 3 p.m.

July 22 Women's and men's individual foil, preliminaries, quarterfinals, semifinals, bronze and gold medals 8 a.m. and 3 p.m.

July 23 Men's team epee, preliminaries, quarterfinals, semifinals, bronze and gold medals 10 a.m. and 3 p.m.

July 24 Women's team epee, preliminaries, quarterfinals and semifinals; men's team sabre, preliminaries, quarterfinals and semifinals 8 a.m. and 3 p.m.

July 25 Women's and men's team foil preliminaries, quarterfinals, semifinals, bronze and gold medals 8 a.m. and 3 p.m.

Gymnastics

Artistic
Georgia Dome
Training
Tickets $11-$22

July 15 Men's compulsory training 11 a.m.
July 16 Women's compulsory training 12 p.m.
July 17 Men's optional training 11 a.m.
July 18 Women's optional training 12 p.m.

Competition
Tickets $27-$265

July 20 Men's team compulsories 9:15 a.m.
July 21 Women's team compulsories 9:30 a.m.
July 22 Men's team optionals and final 9:15 a.m.
July 23 Women's team optionals and final 9:30 a.m.
July 24 Men's individual all-around final 4:15 p.m.
July 25 Women's individual all-around final 4:15 p.m.
July 28 Men's floor exercise final, men's pommel horse final, men's rings final, women's vault final, women's uneven bars final 9:30 p.m.
July 29 Men's vault final, men's parallel bars final, men's high bars final, women's floor exercise final 7:30 p.m.

July 30 Gymnastics exhibition 4 p.m.

Rhythmic
University of Georgia, Athens
Tickets $25-$53

Aug. 1 Individual and group preliminaries 10 a.m.
Aug. 2 Individual preliminaries and group finals 10 a.m.
Aug. 3 Individual semifinals 10 a.m.
Aug. 4 Individual finals 1 p.m.

Handball
Georgia World Congress Center, Georgia Dome
Tickets $16-$27

July 24 Men's preliminaries 10 a.m.
July 25 Men's preliminaries 10 a.m.
July 26 Women's preliminaries 10 a.m.
July 27 Men's preliminaries 10 a.m.
July 28 Women's preliminaries 10 a.m.
July 29 Men's preliminaries 10 a.m.
July 30 Women's preliminaries 10 a.m.
July 31 Men's preliminaries 10 a.m.
Aug. 1 Women's semifinals and classification 10 a.m.
Aug. 2 Men's semifinals and classification 10 a.m.
Aug. 3 Women's bronze and gold medal 3:30 p.m.
Aug. 4 Men's bronze and gold medal 3 p.m.

Field Hockey
Atlanta University Center
Tickets $11-$27

July 20 Men's and women's preliminaries 8:30 a.m.
July 21 Men's and women's preliminaries 9 a.m.
July 22 Men's and women's preliminaries 9 a.m.
July 23 Men's and women's preliminaries 8:30 a.m.
July 24 Men's and women's preliminaries 9 a.m.
July 25 Men's and women's preliminaries 8:30 a.m.
July 26 Men's and women's preliminaries 8:30 a.m.
July 27 Men's and women's preliminaries 8:30 a.m.
July 28 Men's and women's preliminaries 8:30 a.m.
July 29 Men's and women's preliminaries 9 a.m.
July 30 Women's preliminaries 9 a.m.
July 31 Men's classification and semifinals 8:30 a.m.
Aug. 1 Women's bronze and gold medals, classification 8:30 a.m.
Aug. 2 Men's bronze and gold medals, classification 9 a.m.

Judo
Georgia World Congress Center
Tickets $22-$43

July 20 Women's heavyweight (over 72kg) and men's heavyweight (over 95kg) preliminaries, repechages, finals 9:30 a.m. and 3 p.m.
July 21 Women's half-heavyweight (72kg) and men's half-heavyweight (95kg) and preliminaries, repechages, finals 9:30 a.m. and 3 p.m.
July 22 Women's middleweight (66kg) and men's middleweight (86kg) preliminaries, repechages, finals 9:30 a.m. and 3 p.m.

July 23 Women's half-middleweight (61kg) and men's half-middleweight (78kg) preliminaries, repechages, finals 9:30 a.m. and 3 p.m.
July 24 Women's lightweight (56kg) and men's lightweight (71kg) preliminaries, repechages, finals 9:30 a.m. and 3 p.m.
July 25 Women's half-lightweight (51kg) and men's half-lightweight (65kg) preliminaries, repechages, finals 9:30 a.m. and 3 p.m.
July 26 Women's extra-lightweight (48kg) and men's extra-lightweight (60kg) preliminaries, repechages, finals 9:30 a.m. and 3 p.m.

Modern Pentathlon
Multiple sites
Tickets $27

July 30 finals, shooting 7:30 a.m.; fencing 9:15 a.m.; swimming 1:45 p.m.; riding 5 p.m.; running 7 p.m.

Rowing
Lake Lanier, Gainesville, Ga.
Tickets $11-$32

July 21 Men's and women's heats 9 a.m.
July 22 Men's and women's heats 9 a.m.
July 23 Men's and women's repechages 9 a.m.
July 24 Men's and women's repechages 9 a.m.
July 25 Men's and women's semifinals 9 a.m.
July 26 Men's and women's semifinals 9 a.m.
July 27 Finals, men's and women's coxless pairs, men's and women's double sculls, men's coxless fours, men's and women's single sculls, 9 a.m.
July 28 Finals, men's and women's light double sculls, men's lightweight coxless fours, men's and women's quadruple sculls, men's and women's eights, 9 a.m.

Shooting
Wolf Creek Shooting Complex
Tickets $22

July 20 Women's 10m air rifle preliminaries and final, men's trap preliminaries, men's 10m air pistol preliminaries and final 9 a.m.
July 21 Men's trap preliminaries and final, women's 10m air pistol preliminaries and final 9 a.m.
July 22 Men's 10m air rifle preliminaries and final 10 a.m.
July 23 Men's 50m free pistol preliminaries and final, women's double trap preliminaries and final 9 a.m.
July 24 Women's 50m 3X20 rifle preliminaries and final, men's double trap preliminaries and final, men's 25m rapid fire pistol preliminaries and final 8:30 a.m.
July 25 Men's 50m prone rifle preliminaries and final, men's 10m run target preliminaries, men's 25m rapid fire pistol preliminaries and final 8:30 a.m.

July 26 Women's 25m sport pistol preliminaries and final, men's 10m run target prelims and final, men's skeet preliminaries 8:30 a.m.

July 27 Men's 50m 3X40 rifle preliminaries and final, men's skeet preliminaries and final 8:30 a.m.

Soccer
Tickets $20-$133
Preliminaries
RFK Stadium, Washington, D.C.

July 20 Men's 3 p.m.
July 21 Men's and women's 3 p.m.
July 22 Men's 7:30 p.m.
July 23 Men's and women's 6:30 p.m.
July 24 Men's 7:30 p.m.
July 25 Men's and women's 6:30 p.m.

Citrus Bowl, Orlando, Fla.

July 20 Men's 6:30 p.m.
July 21 Men's and women's 4 p.m.
July 22 Men's 7 p.m.
July 23 Men's and women's 6 p.m.
July 24 Men's 7 p.m.
July 25 Men's and women's 6:30 p.m.

Legion Field, Birmingham, Ala.

July 20 Men's 7:30 p.m.
July 21 Men's and women's 2:30 p.m.
July 22 Men's 6:30 p.m.
July 23 Men's and women's 5:30 p.m.
July 24 Men's 6:30 p.m.
July 25 Men's and women's 6:30 p.m.

Quarterfinals
Legion Field, Birmingham, Ala.

July 27 Men's 7:30 p.m.
July 28 Men's 4 p.m.

Orange Bowl, Miami

July 27 Men's 6 p.m.
July 28 Men's 6 p.m.

Semifinals
University of Georgia, Athens

July 28 Women's 3 p.m.
July 31 Men's 3 p.m.

Medal Rounds
University of Georgia, Athens, Ga.

Aug. 1 Women's bronze and gold medals 6 p.m.
Aug. 2 Men's bronze medal 8 p.m.
Aug. 3 Men's gold medal 3:30 p.m.

Softball
Columbus, Ga.
Tickets $16-$32

July 21 Preliminaries 9 a.m. and 6:30 p.m.
July 22 Preliminaries 9 a.m. and 6:30 p.m.
July 23 Preliminaries 9 a.m. and 6:30 p.m.
July 24 Preliminaries 9 a.m. and 6:30 p.m.
July 25 Preliminaries 9 a.m. and 6:30 p.m.
July 26 Preliminaries 9 a.m. and 6:30 p.m.
July 27 Preliminaries 9 a.m. and 6:30 p.m.
July 29 Semifinals 6:30 p.m.
July 30 Bronze and gold medals 4:30 p.m.

Swimming
Georgia Tech
Tickets $27-$159

July 20 Women's 100-meter freestyle, men's 100 breaststroke, women's 400 individual medley, men's 200 free, preliminaries 10:05 a.m., finals 7:33 p.m.

July 21 Women's 200 free, men's 400 IM, women's 100 breast, men's 4X200 free relay, preliminaries 10:05 a.m., finals 7:33.

July 22 Women's 400 free, men's 100 free, women's 100 backstrokes 200 butterfly, women's 4X100 free relay, preliminaries 10:05 a.m., finals 7:33.

July 23 Men's 400 free, women's 200 breast, men's 100 back, women's 100 fly, men's 4X100 free relay, preliminaries 10:05 a.m., finals 7:33.

July 24 Men's 200 breast, women's 200 IM, men's 100 fly, women's 4X100 medley relay, preliminaries 10:05 a.m., finals 7:33; women's 800 free, preliminaries 10:05 a.m.

July 25 Men's 50 free, women's 200 back, men's 200 medley, women's 4 by 200 free, preliminaries 10:05 a.m., finals 7:33 p.m.; men's 1500 free, preliminaries 10:05 a.m.; women's 800 free finals, 7:33 p.m.

July 26 Women's 200 fly, men's 200 back, women's 50 free, men's 4 by 100 medley, preliminaries 10:05 a.m., finals 7:33 p.m.; men's 1500 free, finals 7:33 p.m.

Synchronized Swimming
Georgia Tech
Tickets $11-$48

July 30 Team preliminaries 10 a.m.
Aug. 2. Team finals 5 p.m.

Table Tennis
Georgia World Congress Center
Tickets $11-$27

July 23 Women's and men's doubles preliminaries 10:30 a.m.

July 24 Women's singles preliminaries 10:30 a.m.

July 25 Women's and men's doubles preliminaries, men's singles preliminaries 10 a.m.

July 26 Men's and women's singles preliminaries, women's doubles quarterfinal, men's singles preliminaries 10 a.m.

July 27 Men's singles preliminaries, women's singles octos, men's doubles quarterfinal, women's doubles semifinals 10 a.m.

July 28 Men's singles octos 10 a.m.

July 29 Women's doubles final, women's singles quarterfinal, men's doubles semifinal 1 p.m.

July 30 Men's doubles final, men's singles quarterfinal, women's singles semifinal 1 p.m.

July 31 Women's singles final, Men's singles semifinal 4:30 p.m.

Aug. 1 Men's singles final 4:30 p.m.

Tennis
Stone Mountain, Ga.
Tickets $27-$132

July 23 Men's and women's singles preliminaries 10 a.m.

July 24 Men's and women's singles preliminaries 10 a.m.

July 25 Men's and women's singles and doubles preliminaries 10 a.m.

July 26 Men's and women's singles and doubles preliminaries 10 a.m.

July 27 Men's and women's singles and doubles preliminaries 10 a.m.

July 28 Men's singles and doubles preliminaries 10 a.m.

July 29 Women's singles and men's doubles quarterfinal 10 a.m.

July 30 Men's singles and women's doubles quarterfinal 11 a.m.

July 31 Women's singles, women's and men's doubles, semifinals 11 a.m.

Aug. 1 Men's singles semifinal; women's and men's doubles bronze medal 11 a.m.

Aug. 2 Women's singles bronze and gold medals, men's doubles gold medal 10 a.m.

Aug. 3 Men's singles bronze and gold medals, women's doubles gold medal

Beach Volleyball
Atlanta Beach, Clayton County, Ga.
Tickets $27-$69

July 23 Women's and men's preliminaries 9 a.m. and 2 p.m.

July 24 Women's and men's preliminaries 9 a.m. and 2 p.m.

July 25 Women's and men's preliminaries 9 a.m. and 2 p.m.

July 26 Women's and men's preliminaries, women's semifinal 9 a.m. and 2 p.m.

July 27 Men's semifinal, women's bronze and gold medals 10 a.m. and 2 p.m.

July 28 Men's bronze and gold medals 11:30 a.m.

Volleyball
University of Georgia and Omni Coliseum
Tickets $16-$133

July 20 Women's preliminaries 10 a.m., 4 p.m., 7:30 p.m.

July 21 Men's preliminaries 10 a.m., 4 p.m., 7:30 p.m.

July 22 Women's preliminaries 10 a.m., 4 p.m., 7:30 p.m.

July 23 Men's preliminaries 10 a.m., 4 p.m., 7:30 p.m.

July 24 Women's preliminaries 10 a.m., 4 p.m., 7:30 p.m.

July 25 Men's preliminaries 10 a.m., 4 p.m., 7:30 p.m.

July 26 Women's preliminaries 10 a.m., 4 p.m., 7:30 p.m.

July 27 Men's preliminaries 10 a.m., 4 p.m., 7:30 p.m.

July 28 Women's preliminaries 10 a.m., 4 p.m., 7:30 p.m.

July 29 Men's preliminaries 10 a.m., 4 p.m., 7:30 p.m.

July 30 Women's quarterfinals 7:30 p.m.

July 31 Men's classification and quarterfinals, noon and 7:30 p.m.

Aug. 1 Women's classification and semifinals, noon and 7:30 p.m.

Aug. 2 Men's classification and semifinals noon and 7:30 p.m.

Aug. 3 Women's bronze and gold medals noon

Aug. 4 Men's bronze and gold medals noon

Water Polo
Georgia Tech
Tickets $11-32

July 20 Preliminaries 11 a.m., 3:30 p.m., 8:30 p.m.

July 21 Preliminaries 11 a.m., 3:30 p.m., 8:30 p.m.

July 22 Preliminaries 11 a.m., 3:30 p.m., 8:30 p.m.

July 23 Preliminaries 11 a.m., 3:30 p.m., 8:30 p.m.

July 24 Preliminaries 11 a.m., 3:30 p.m., 8:30 p.m.

July 26 Preliminaries 10:30 a.m., 4 p.m., 8:30 p.m.

July 27 Classification and semifinals 11 a.m., 3:30 p.m., 8:30 p.m.

July 28 Classifications 8 a.m. and 11:30 a.m.; bronze and gold medals 3 p.m.

Weightlifting
Georgia World Congress Center
Tickets $22-$43

July 20 54kg Group B 12:30 p.m., Group A 3:30 p.m.

July 21 59kg Group B 12:30 p.m., Group A 3:30 p.m.

July 22 64kg Group B 12:30 p.m., Group A 3:30 p.m.

July 23 70kg Group B 12:30 p.m., Group A 3:30 p.m.

July 24 76kg Group B 12:30 p.m., Group A 3:30 p.m.

July 26 83kg Group B 12:30 p.m., Group A 3:30 p.m.

July 27 91kg Group B 12:30 p.m., Group A 3:30 p.m.

July 28 99kg Group B 12:30 p.m., Group A 3:30 p.m.

July 29 108kg Group B 12:30 p.m., Group A 3:30 p.m.

July 30 over 108kg Group B 12:30 p.m., Group A 3:30 p.m.

Wrestling
Georgia World Congress Center
Tickets $22-$43
Freestyle

July 30 48kg, 57kg, 68kg, 82kg, and 100kg preliminaries and classification 9:30 a.m. and 3:30 p.m.

July 31 48kg, 57kg, 68kg, 82kg, and 100kg classification, bronze and gold medals 9:30 a.m. and 3:30 p.m.

Aug. 1 52kg, 62kg, 74kg, 90kg, 130kg preliminaries and classification 9:30 a.m. and 3:30 p.m.

Aug. 2   52kg, 62kg, 74kg, 90kg, 130kg classification, bronze and gold medals 9:30 a.m. and 3:30 p.m.

Greco-Roman

July 20   48kg, 57kg, 68kg, 82kg, and 100kg preliminaries and classification 9:30 a.m. and 3:30 p.m.

July 21   48kg, 57kg, 68kg, 82kg, and 100kg classification, bronze and gold medals 9:30 a.m. and 3:30 p.m.

July 22   52kg, 62kg, 74kg, 90kg, 130kg preliminaries and classification 9:30 a.m. and 3:30 p.m.

July 23   52kg, 62kg, 74kg, 90kg, 130kg classification, bronze and gold medals 9:30 a.m. and 3:30 p.m.

Yachting

Wassaw Sound, Savannah, Ga.
Ticket prices TBD

July 22   Men's and women's Mistral, men's and women's 470, Star, Finn 1 p.m.

July 23   Men's and women's Mistral, men's and women's 470, Star, Finn 1 p.m.

July 24   Men's and women's Mistral, men's and women's 470, Star, Finn, Soling, Tornado 1 p.m.

July 25   Laser, Europe, Soling, Tornado 1 p.m.

July 26   Laser, Europe, Star, Finn, Soling, Tornado 1 p.m.

July 27   Men's and women's Mistral, Laser, Europe, Star, Finn, Soling, Tornado 1 p.m.

July 28   Men's and women's Mistral, Men's and women's 470, Star finals, Finn finals, Soling 1 p.m.

July 29   Men's and women's Mistral finals, men's and women's 470, Laser, Europe, Tornado 1 p.m.

July 30   Men's and women's 470 finals, Laser, Europe, Tornado finals

July 31   Soling match races, Laser finals, Europe finals 1 p.m.

Aug. 1   Soling match race finals 1 p.m.

Closing Ceremony

Olympic Stadium
Tickets $212-$636
Aug. 4 9 p.m.

CHAPTER XVII

The Olympic Champions

ABOVE: Bonnie Blair, after winning the gold medal in the Olympic 500-meter speedskating in 1994.

You might think by the time you got to gold medal No. 5, it would be old hat, just another trinket to collect dust or clutter a dresser drawer. But look at this:

RIGHT: Jim Thorpe, shown here in the uniform of his Carlisle Indian School, won the 1912 Olympic decathlon, a title later stripped for violating the amateurs-only code.

Here's Bonnie Blair, the winningest American woman in Olympic history, and she has her latest two gold medals draped around her neck, her fourth and fifth, collected this time in a spectacular Norwegian ice hall that looks like an overturned Viking ship.

And she's staring at the medals the way a kid on Christmas morning stares at a new bicycle.

There's a look of, "I can't quite believe this," on the face of the 23-year-old speedskater from West Allis, Wisconsin. As she sits with a group of reporters, answering questions toward the end of the 1994 Winter Games in Lillehammer, she occasionally glances down at the heavy circles of Norwegian granite with the gilt rims. Unconsciously, the thumb and forefinger of her right hand caress the medals and gently rub them, reassurance that these are for real, just like the one Blair won in Calgary in 1988 and the two she picked up in Albertville, France, in '92.

Blair is a tough, wise, veteran athlete who battled the best in her sport for more than a decade and came out on top. But those medals inspire awe even in the people who collect them, more for what they represent than what they are.

"There is no job, no amount of power, no money to approach the Olympic experience," said Al Oerter, a four-time Olympic champion in the most classic of all field events, the discus.

Oerter was a world-class competitor for almost three decades and is now a successful businessman, but he is known best for his Olympic feats. It is that way with most athletes who—through persistence and training and sacrifice and skill and even a little bit of luck—stand on the highest tier of the medal podium and have the gold medal placed around their neck as the crowd cheers and their national anthem is played.

The medal and the cheers for a long time were the only rewards for Olympians. Money was made from the Games, but the athletes dared not touch it, as the tragic case of Jim Thorpe showed.

The amateur-only rules were not limited to the Olympics when Coubertin revived the Games in 1896. Virtually all sports were for those who played for the sheer love of the game—in French, "l'amateur" is "the lover." And where some played for pay, they were generally considered to be on the lower scale. English cricket, perhaps the sport most strictly defined by class, separated its contestants into professional "players" and amateur "gentlemen," and the two sides never met.

This led to blatant hypocrisy, with athletes accepting under-the-table payments so they could both eat and preserve their amateur status. The East bloc built state-run sports factories, churning out athletes who were pure professionals but got around the ban by holding shadow "jobs" as soldiers or physical culture students.

The Olympic Charter, the bylaws of the IOC and the rules upon which the whole community is based, specifically limited the Games to amateurs for the first seven decades. But in 1971, the word "amateur" was stripped from the charter. That opened the door to professionals, although it would be another 13 years before the first—a few minor league ice hockey players—actually took part.

But it was tennis that provided the real opening for a wide-open Olympics, with competition among the best athletes—be they amateurs or pros.

Tennis was dropped from the Games after 1924 and readmitted as a one-time-only demonstration sport in Los Angeles 60 years later. A couple of young, relatively unknown players named Steffi Graf and Stefan Edberg won the women's and men's singles titles, and the success of the exhibition forced the IOC to consider retaining tennis as a full medal sport in 1988. One problem: The International Tennis Federation wanted the Olympic tournament to have the best players, not just college stars or other amateurs. That meant that some of the world's highest-paid athletes, multimillionaires such as Boris Becker and, by then, Graf, would tread the Olympic paths. That prospect was too much for many IOC members, who feared that the superstars would hide away in five-star hotels and emerge only to play matches in return for lucrative endorsement deals with sponsors.

But Juan Antonio Samaranch, who took over as IOC president in 1980, was a big tennis fan and eager to open the Games to the best athletes in all sports. So he drew up a list of restrictions and regulations that any professional athlete would have to agree to before being declared eligible for the Olympic tournament. Among other things, they would be barred from making any money directly from their Olympic performance and they had to live with the rest of the athletes in the Olympic Village.

This latter provision was largely symbolic. There was no way to force an athlete to live in the usually cramped, spartan confines of the village dorm rooms or to prevent them from checking into the village and actually living in a posh hotel or private villa nearby. But the act was enough to sway even the fiercest critics of the new "open" Olympics.

"If an athlete agrees to sleep on the hard bed of the Olympic Village, my friend, he is a true Olympian," declared the Comte de Beaumont, a regal Frenchman and one of the IOC's old guard, as he and the rest of the committee voted in May 1987 to allow pro tennis players in Seoul.

From there, it was goodbye poorhouse, hello Dream Team.

Graf became only the second woman to sweep tennis' Grand Slam when she won the Australian, French and U.S. Opens and Wimbledon in 1988, but her accomplishments were not complete until she won the Olympic women's singles title in Seoul—her "Golden Slam."

Amateur or pro, to be an Olympic champion is to be more than an athlete. It is to represent the finest in the human spirit—the will to do your best, to follow the rules, to care for others and to give something back to your fellow man and woman. To win a gold medal, you must break barriers, not just in speed and weight and distance but often socially and culturally ways as well. You must accept the responsibility of being the best as the whole world watches.

It would be impossible to pick out the ultimate Olympic champion. Each has a unique claim to lasting fame. But here are five gold medalists who transcended their sports, who in some way did something that never had been done before, who grabbed the attention of billions of people and added to the image of the ultimate athlete.

SEBASTIAN COE

You could measure Sebastian Coe's success in many ways.

As a politician, who rose quickly through the ranks of Britain's Conservative Party to win a seat in the House of Commons.

As an advocate, one of the first world-class athletes to speak out loudly against the dangers of performance-enhancing drugs.

As a veteran runner, with nine world records to his credit, including one that stood for more than a decade.

But there are three races by which Coe's career will always be remembered, and all three came in the Olympics.

ABOVE: The British Union Jack is displayed by Sebastian Coe after his victory in the 1,500 meters in Los Angeles.

With the United States leading a boycott of the 1980 Games in Moscow to protest Soviet military intervention in Afghanistan, the Olympics were searching for a hook—something or someone that would make the Games more than just a competition of East bloc athletes.

It found that hook in Coe and his British rival, Steve Ovett, the two greatest middle-distance runners of the era.

Coe and Ovett were not friends. They came from different backgrounds and supported different political interests. And each knew that the other was keeping him from being acclaimed the best.

They avoided each other on the track for two years, all the while setting records in the mile, the 1,500 meters, the 800 meters, the 1,000 meters and the two-mile—15 world marks in all.

Finally, in Moscow, they would have to run against each other, and what races they would be.

The 800 was first. Coe, the world record-holder, was favored, and breezed through the first round and the semifinals. But in the final, the little man from north London, known as a master of strategy, ran what he would later describe as "the worst race of my life."

After 400 meters, Coe was dead last in the eight-man field. Ovett was in trouble in the middle of the pack, but fought his way to the front in the final lap in a flurry of swinging elbows and lunging strides. Coe could do nothing right. Unable to fight through the field, he veered to the outside lanes and couldn't make up the lost time.

Ovett won the gold medal in 1:45.4, well off Coe's world mark of 1:42.33. Coe was second in 1:45.9, just .10 seconds ahead of bronze medalist Nikolai Kirov of the Soviet Union.

"I suppose I must have compounded more cardinal sins of middle-distance running in 1 ½ minutes than I've done in a lifetime," Coe said after the 800. "I've got to come back and climb the mountain again. The 1,500 was going to be a hard event anyway, but now it's going to be the big race of my life. I must win it."

Pressure does strange things to athletes. It can push them to their greatest glories, or it can drag them down to ignominious defeat.

Coe would not let pressure—or Ovett—beat him again.

Coe and Ovett shared the world record in the 1,500, at 3:32.1, and Ovett entered the Olympic final with a heady psychological advantage.

In the week between the 800 disappointment and the race for perhaps the Olympics' ultimate track title, that advantage seemed to grow. Coe was sluggish in the heats and took brutal criticism from British writers, who were saying that he was a record-setting machine who lacked the fire and guts to win gold medals.

So Coe went out to prove the world wrong. When the gun sounded to start the 1,500, Coe surged to the front, where his tactical mastery could be used to greatest advantage. After a 61.6-second first lap, Coe settled in just behind Jurgen Straub of East Germany, with Ovett over his shoulder. Just past the halfway mark, Straub accelerated, and Coe and his father-coach, Peter, liked the move.

"I found a rhythm, a lane of my own," the runner said. Added the coach: "No one in the world can sustain that speed as Seb can."

With 200 meters remaining, it was Straub by four yards over Coe and six over Ovett. As they neared the final turn, Coe moved outside and into the lead, with Ovett clinging to his back. But here Coe found more speed and pulled away, completing the race in 3:38.4 with a 52.1 final lap—and final 100 meters in 12.1. Straub was second, .40 seconds behind, and Ovett took the bronze another .20 seconds back.

No distance runner looks good at the end of a race and the picture of Coe crossing the finish line of the Moscow 1,500 shows a man who appears to be in the throes of a seizure. His mouth and jaws are clenched. His neck muscle bulge. His eyes are big and white, and seem about to roll over in his head. His arms are spread wide, perhaps grasping for help.

This was an Olympic champion? It sure was.

Coe knelt and touched his head to the track, then took a victory lap. "Perhaps somebody, somewhere, loves me after all," Coe said.

Coe would cap his next Olympic gold medal with a very different gesture, one containing not a bit of love.

Medical problems plagued Coe after his gold medal victory in Moscow. He suffered back pains, a bout of glandular fever, under surgery for removal of a lymph node and was diagnosed with toxoplasmosis. He had to withdraw from the first World Track and Field Championships in 1983. As the new Olympic year approached, track writers were saying openly that Coe's days as a world-beater were done.

Coe would not listen. He resumed training in December 1983 and made the British Olympic team despite losing to a rising star, Peter Elliott, in the national championships, a selection that was scorned by the nation's press.

By the time the Olympics arrived in Los Angeles in the summer of 1984, Ovett held the world 1,500 meter record of 3:30.77. And there was another Steve on the British track circuit—Steve Cram, who won the 1,500 world championship the previous summer.

Coe was determined, however, to show he was still king of metric milers, and the LA Olympic race would be the perfect spot to do it. It turned into a race of attrition even before the start of qualifying, with Said Aouita and Sydney Maree dropping out. Ovett collapsed in the 800-meter final—where Coe won silver again—and required hospitalization for chest pains but made the 1,500 field.

The final was a strange race. Coe broke to the front from the gun but quickly gave up the lead to Omar Khalifa of the Sudan. Less than halfway into the race, American Steve Scott surged to the front, trying to avoid a last-lap kick contest that he knew he could not win. The field followed him, with Coe and Cram near the front and Jose Abascal of Spain right with

Right: Babe Didrikson, perhaps the greatest woman athlete of all time, prior to winning the javelin at the Los Angeles Games in 1932.

them. Scott began to fade as Abascal took the lead, and Ovett dropped out of the race with about a lap to go as the mysterious chest pains came again. Coe and Cram kept at it, tearing by Abascal on the final turn. Coe led by about a yard at the top of the stretch and pulled away to beat Cram in an Olympic-record 3:32.53.

This time, the finish line brought a huge smile to Coe's face. He turned to his right, and looked up into the press stands where his severest critics sat. Waving his fingers derisively, Coe shouted: "Who says I'm finished?"

That was the finish of Coe's Olympic career. By 1988 he was no longer an elite runner and had his mind more on politics than sports. After failing to qualify for the British team for Seoul, Coe was offered an unprecedented wild-card berth in the Olympic 1,500 by IOC President Samaranch, an offer that was widely criticized and later withdrawn.

But Coe had his mark in history. He was the first man to win two consecutive gold medals in the Olympic 1,500.

BABE DIDRIKSON

She could type 85 words per minute. Her sewing was so good it won the blue ribbon at the Texas State Fair. And boy, could she play the harmonica.

Mildred "Babe" Didrikson could do all of that—and much, much more. She was perhaps the greatest female athlete of all time, and her impact on sports in general was immense.

For the Olympics, Didrikson was a liberating force still difficult to imagine.

Women were little more than an after-thought in the early years of the modern Games. Coubertin had no time for women's sports and with few exceptions that philosophy carried through the 1920s, when the Games slowly opened to female athletes. Suzanne Lenglen won the women's tennis gold medal in Paris in 1924, but her feats at Wimbledon and Roland Garros were much better known. Sonja Heine made her Olympic debut in figure skating in 1924 and won a gold

medal four years later, but she was considered a novelty act, not a true athlete.

Didrikson changed all of that in Los Angeles in 1932. No one who watched her compete could deny having seen a performer with superb athletic ability.

She was born in Port Arthur, Texas, the town that later would produce Janis Joplin and Jimmy Johnson. Like them, she combined pure talent with showmanship. She was good, and she let people know it.

"I am out to beat everybody in sight," Didrikson said as she headed to the Los Angeles Games. "And that's just what I'm going to do."

Sports fans knew of Didrikson long before Los Angeles. She was an All-American basketball player who also excelled in baseball, swimming, diving and even billiards. She was a track star so good that, when the women's Olympic team was picked in one-day trials at Northwestern University on July 4, 1932,

Didrikson took part in eight events—and won six. She set world records in the javelin, high jump and 80-meter hurdles and also won the baseball throw, shot put and long jump. She was a one-woman team, representing the Employees Casualty Insurance Co., of Dallas, where she worked as a typist, and her total points won the team championship. The 22-woman squad from the University of Illinois was second.

Limited by Olympic rules to three events in Los Angeles, Didrikson chose her three world-record specialties. Good choices. She won the javelin with a throw of 143 feet, 4 inches and the hurdles in a world-record 11.7 seconds. It appeared she won the high jump in a jump-off against U.S. teammate Jean Shirley, with both clearing a world-record 5-5 ¾, but officials disqualified Didrikson for diving over the crossbar and gave Shirley the gold medal. Unlike most jumpers who straddled the bar with a high scissors kick, Didrikson used the Western roll, where the head is down and body follows. The Western roll was legalized shortly after the Games. It was just one more case where Didrikson was ahead of her time.

Although Los Angeles made her the first true Olympic women's superstar, Didrikson never competed in the Games again. Like Jim Thorpe, she was barred for violating the simon pure rules of amateurism, in her case for endorsing a car company. Because the situation occurred after her Olympic success, she was not stripped of her medals or records. And even though the nation was gripped by the Depression, Didrikson found financial success in sports, although in sometimes unorthodox ways.

She toured the vaudeville circuit, playing harmonica, telling jokes and demonstrating her shot put form. She played with the barnstorming baseball team from the House of David, a bearded Jewish sect with a squad that also featured occasional appearances by Babe Ruth. It was while she was on the road that she met her husband—a little unorthodox, too, in keeping with Didrikson's style.

George Zaharias was a professional wrestler, a 285-pound behemoth promoted as the "Crying Greek from Cripple Creek." He encouraged his new wife to concentrate on golf, and once again she became one of the best that ever was.

From 1946 to '47, Babe Didrikson Zaharias won 14 straight tournaments. She won the U.S. Women's Amateur title in 1946 and became the first U.S. winner of the British Women's Amateur the following year. In 1948 she turned pro and won the first of three U.S. Women's Opens and the first of four straight World Championships. Her purse winnings of $14,800 in 1950 was a world record for a woman golfer.

That was the year that Didrikson was voted the Female Athlete of the Half-Century in an AP poll. But it wasn't long before tragedy struck. Didriken was diagnosed with cancer of the colon in 1953 and underwent an emergency colostomy. She returned to golf 3 ½ months later, winning a minor tournament, and won the U.S. Women's Open by 12 strokes the following year.

The comeback was not to last. The cancer returned. Mildred "Babe" Didrikson Zaharias was 42 when she died on September 17, 1956, in Galveston, Texas.

MARK SPITZ

Remember the poster? This big guy, handsome and tanned, dark hair modishly long, moustache bristling over pearly white teeth, a skimpy swimsuit guarding his loins.

And around his neck hung seven—count 'em, SEVEN—Olympic gold medals.

A generation before kids wanted to be like Mike, they wanted to be like Mark.

Mark Spitz was the megahero of his day. And why not? What he accomplished in the architecturally stunning swimming hall in Munich may never be equalled, may never even be approached.

Spitz was a brash kid from California who set very high goals for himself. Over and over he was told by his father, "Swimming isn't everything—winning is." This helped him become one of the world's best swimmers by the time the 1968 Olympics opened in Mexico City, but it could also get him into trouble.

Just 18 years old, Spitz predicted that he would leave Mexico with a record six gold medals. Instead, he returned home with just two, both in relays, and the memory of a last-

place finish in his final individual race, the 200-meter butterfly.

Over the next four years, Spitz would set his sights almost demonically on the pool at Munich and making up for his failures in Mexico. When the schedule for the 1972 Games was announced, Spitz knew he would get a chance to redeem himself. The first event on his race calendar was the 200 'fly.

You could see Spitz's determination as he waited on the pool deck for the final of his all-important race to begin. Spitz stared straight ahead, almost willing the water to part. When the gun went off, he sprang forward and churned up the pool, never letting up and winning in 2 minutes, 0.7 seconds, more than two seconds faster than the runner-up, U.S. teammate Gary Hall. To measure how thoroughly Spitz had won and erased the memories of Mexico City, consider this: Hall's time of 2:02.86 would have won every previous Olympic 200 butterfly final by some four seconds.

Spitz leaped from the pool and thrust his hands high. The ghost was gone. The gold rush was on.

An hour later, Spitz was back in the pool, swimming the anchor leg as the U.S. team won the 400-meter freestyle relay in a world-record 3:26.42, almost 2 ½ seconds faster than the old mark.

Next up was the 200 freestyle, and it turned out to be a tough race—with a controversy at the end. Spitz trailed teammate Steve Genter going into the final 50-meter lap. He drove forward and beat Genter by almost a full second to break his own world record in 1:52.78. After receiving gold medal No. 3, Spitz waved his sneakers at the crowd—and the photographers. It took some fast talking by Spitz to convince an IOC inquiry that he was not trying to get publicity for a sponsor but instead merely letting the fans known how happy he was over another victory.

The sneakers were out of sight when Spitz won his next race, the 100 butterfly. A silver-medalist in Mexico City behind teammate

Doug Russell, Spitz this time lowered his own world record to 54.27 and beat Canada's Bruce Robertson by almost 1 ½ seconds, an unbelievable margin in a race so short.

The record for gold medals in the Olympics was five, set by Italian fencer Nedo Nadi in 1920. Spitz tied that mark in the 800-meter freestyle relay, swimming anchor on a 7:35.78 world record. The relay victory came less than an hour after Spitz finished the 100 'fly and gave him five gold medals—and five world records—in four days. The five golds also were one more than the number won in 1964 by Don Schollander, the previous record for an Olympic swimmer.

Two races were left for Spitz—the 100-meter freestyle and the 400-meter medley relay on the final day of swimming. Victory in the medley relay seemed a sure thing, since the American men were dominating the pool. But to remain undefeated, Spitz would have to overcome both a hot swimmer, teammate Jerry Heidenreich, and his own doubts.

Spitz wanted those seven gold medals. But—as his father had stressed—he wanted perfection even more. Six-for-six would, in Spitz's mind, be better than 6-for-7. Rumors circulated that Spitz would drop out of the 100 free.

Those rumors reached Sherm Chavoor, Spitz's coach, who tore into his swimmer. He said Spitz was crazy. He said people would call Spitz "chicken" if he didn't compete.

Spitz swam in the 100 freestyle—and won. He sandbagged Heidenreich and defending champion Michael Wenden of Australian in the heats and semifinals, then departed from his usual tactics by storming to lead in the final and holding off Heidenreich by a half stroke in 51.22, another world record.

Six down. And Spitz finished his seven-race sweep by winning the butterfly leg on the U.S. 400 medley relay. Anchored by Heidenreich's freestyle, the United States won in a world-record 3:48.16.

The performance by Spitz was hailed around the world, although the athlete himself was held in lower regard. On top of his brashness, his flouting of anti-commercial rules and his reputed attempt to duck a tough opponent, Spitz left the Olympics early after the attack by Palestinian terrorists on Israeli coaches and athletes in the Munich Village. Spitz felt that, because he was Jewish and the highest-profile athlete at the Olympics, he was a potential target for attackers. But many critics said Spitz should have stayed with his teammates and fellow Olympians at such a dark moment.

When he got home, Spitz tried to turn his Olympic success into quick cash. The poster was the most obvious effort, with lifesized editions soon on display in stores and decorating the bedrooms of teen-agers nation-wide. Other ventures proved less successful and often embarrassing.

Spitz was a dental student, but now he wanted to become an actor. One of is first appearances was on a TV show with Bob Hope, in which Spitz played a dentist and the comedian was his reluctant patient. The skit was awful, with Spitz coming across wooden and arrogant. A star was not born.

Relations between Spitz and Olympic officials also were cool, and many of the wounds to Spitz were self-inflicted. Despite a lack of success in acting, Spitz found work as a swimming commentator for television, and worked many big meets. One was the 1983

Sports Festival in Colorado Springs, Colorado, part of the U.S. Olympic Committee's program to develop top-class athletes. In an interview before the competition one night, Spitz trashed the festivals, saying they had done very little to bring along Olympic athletes and diverted money from more worthwhile programs. The following year, Spitz became embroiled in another controversy when he said he was unhappy about not being included among the U.S. Olympic champions honored in opening ceremonies at the 1984 Los Angeles Games.

Whatever his shortcomings as a showman or diplomat, Spitz remains the winningest Olympic athlete ever in a single Games. That 7-for-7 is tough to top.

KATARINA WITT

To be an Olympic champion takes more than a life of hard work, dedication and athletic skills. It also helps to be in the right place at the right time.

Katarina Witt made sure that no matter where she skated, that place was her place; that no matter what the time might be, that time was the right time.

Since the Winter Olympics began in 1924, the winner of the women's figure skating gold medal has been someone special. Sonja Heine won three in a row and became a movie star. Carol Heiss traveled from the blue-collar neighborhoods of New York to win a gold for her late mother. Peggy Fleming captivated the world with grace and skill. Dorothy Hamil wowed us with her hairdo and her spins.

But Witt did all this and more. She created her own era and aura, and refined it over and over again.

We first saw her as a kid in Sarajevo, where she was constantly described as a lookalike for Brooke Shields, the supermodel of the time.

Witt was a daughter of East Germany. But even when she beat skaters from the United States and Canada, she somehow humanized the Communist state and had capitalism lapping at her heels.

As she grew up, the image changed from a slim teen-ager denied ice cream and other treats by her coach to a sassy temptress full of

ABOVE: German figure skater Katarina Witt going through her daily practice before the free skating competition in Norway.

Even when she was beating apple pie Americans such as Rosalynn Sumners and Debi Thomas, her success and sex appeal was luring viewers, making figure skating the most-watched event in the Olympics. That attracted sponsors with millions and millions of dollars to spend. And that changed the Olympics forever.

Witt was an Olympic fixture for the better part of 10 years. During that time, she won two gold medals—the first consecutive winner in women's figures since Heine's three in a row from 1928-36—and broke many more hearts.

It could be argued that Witt was not the best skater of her generation, and that she was lucky to win her golds. Her strengths were technical correctness, visual appeal and an iron belief in her ability, forged by coach Jutta Mueller. Witt simply did not make mistakes.

In Sarajevo, for example, Witt was third behind Sumners after the compulsories and led after the short program. Whoever won the free skate would win the gold. Witt skated a controlled program that was strong but not so overpowering to bar the way for Sumners, who was the reigning world champion. But Sumners let up late in her routine, popping out of two multiple jumps, and Witt was the winner.

She was the people's choice, too, receiving 35,000 love letters along with the gold.

Four years later, in Calgary, Witt was the reigning world champion with only one loss since Sarajevo—to Thomas, in the 1986 World Championships. Thomas, a pre-med student from Stanford, was ready to knock the East German off her perch. But this was the Olympics—Katy's place. Again, the time was right.

Thomas led Witt after compulsories and the short program. It was time for the duel of the "Carmens," each skater choosing the Bizet piece for her long program for one of the most anticipated evenings of Olympic competition ever.

Witt appeared in icy blue with a silver tiara. As in Sarajevo, she skated first, and again skated within herself, relying on flawless presentation for high marks. Thomas, in black and silver, had a chance for the gold. But she

mystery. She played off the East-West conflict, saying she was a proud product of socialism.

And then when the Berlin Wall fell and she was shown to be as much of a victim as a beneficiary of the old order, she had the courage and intelligence to make the most of the change and become a spokeswoman for athletes and the oppressed. And through it all, she skated as few others had, always with that feeling of time and place. Heine gave the world its first glimpse of figure skating greatness; Fleming graced the sport with elegance; and Hamil provided the perky, peppy counterpoint to the economic doldrums of the mid-1970s. Witt added sex and sizzle, flash and dash.

popped out of a triple jump barely 20 seconds into her routine and never recovered her composure, finishing third behind Canada's Elizabeth Manley.

Again, Witt had won. And again, there was love interest. This time it was skier Alberto Tomba, a double-gold medalist from Italy, who waited—in vain—with red roses for the two-time champion.

It soon became known that other people were waiting for Witt, as well. No skater ever travels alone, but Witt's entourage included members of the Stassi, the East German secret police. When communism crumbled in her homeland, the release of Stassi files showed Witt and other East German athletes had been used by the state as apologists and propagandists, and kept under constant surveillance at home and abroad. Witt wrote in her autobiography that Stassi agents even timed her and her boyfriend as they had sex.

With barriers to the West down, Witt toured with professional ice shows and produced television skating specials with other Olympic champions such as Brian Boitano. Like many former athletes, she tried her hand as a television commentator, working with CBS at the 1992 Winter Games in Albertville, France. As many other ex-jocks found, it's not easy to transform what you did in front of the cameras to expert analysis, and a lasting memory of Witt at those Olympics may be of the two-time gold medalist sitting, alone and crying, in a bar in Moutiers, France, the night of her birthday.

When the Winter Games went to a different Olympic cycle and the International Skating Union changed its rules to allow professionals to re-apply for Olympic eligibility, Witt decided to give it one last shot at Lillehammer in 1994. She was 28, and judging now favored jumping ability and athleticism over style and grace, so her chances of winning a medal were remote. But Witt was still a star. The Lillehammer crowd roared for her as Robin Hood in the short program and cheered her salute to Sarajevo, the war-torn site of her first Olympic success, in the finale.

She finished seventh, but what did it matter? Witt wanted that chance to say goodbye, and acknowledge how important the Olympics had been to her and what even an oldtimer can do.

"I wanted to demonstrate, and I did, that one can motivate oneself, even when one is already 28 years old and knows that one cannot win a medal," she said. "I dedicated time to it, but I'm proud of having done it again and that people understood what I wanted to express. For me, it was important to emphasize the message of peace of the Olympic Games."

NADIA COMANECI

Perfection.

The Olympic motto talks about moving faster, soaring higher, being stronger. It recognizes human frailty in what it omits. Perfection, in the Olympian's eye, is something to strive for, never attain.

So if sprinter Linford Christie was faster, and pole vaulter Sergei Bubka was higher, and weightlifter Vassily Alexeyev was stronger, what did Nadia Comaneci represent?

That's easy. Nadia was perfect.

In a gymnastics arena in Montreal in 1976, Comaneci showed the world that speed and height and strength were not the only things that could be measured. So could unspoiled movement, graceful yet frightening in its twists and flips and turns.

Comaneci took gymnastics to uncharted territory. Building on a legacy of great gymnasts form Eastern Europe such as Vera Caslavska of Czechoslovakia and Lyudmilla Tourischeva and Olga Korbut of the Soviet Union, Comaneci forced her sport through new frontiers and left it in the mainstream, for millions of teen-age girls worldwide to dream of tumbling in her slippers.

Such a feat for someone so young and so small.

Comaneci was 14 years old, standing an inch under 5 feet and weighing 86 pounds, when she arrived in Montreal from Romania as the favorite for the women's all-around title. There was good reason for that status. For one, Comaneci had an eight-year winning streak. For another, she held in her a fire that burned to win and, as it turned out, to survive.

She was plucked from a school playground by coach Bela Karolyi as a 6-year-old. One of

ABOVE: Perfection itself! Nadia Comaneci salutes the crowd in Montreal after her third perfect 10 in the 1976 Games, this one on the uneven bars.

her first competitions resulted in a 13th-place finish—and Karolyi's warning that she must never finish 13th again. Karolyi also gave her an Eskimo doll, which she carried to Montreal.

Gym freaks had heard of Comaneci and her outspoken coach, Karolyi. Most others, however, were focused on Korbut, the Soviet sprite who had dazzled the world in Munich, and Tourischeva, the defending all-around champion.

It didn't take long, however, for Comaneci to make herself known—and for the Olympics and gymnastics to see something that not even the mathematicians had envisioned.

With a capacity crowd of 16,000 settling into its seats at the Montreal Forum on July 19, 1976, Comaneci began her routine on the uneven bars. For 90 seconds she whirled and twirled in a gymnastic never-never land.

Montreal was wired for state-of-the-art scoreboards. But the state of the gymnastics art stopped at 9.9.

Until that night.

Comaneci was awarded a perfect 10—the first in Olympic history.

By the time Comaneci returned to the arena, the computer experts had corrected their gaffe and fixed the scoreboard to show two digits to the left of the decimal. That was a good thing.

Comaneci received a total of seven 10s in Montreal, and won gold medals in the uneven bars, the balance beam and the all-around.

"I am here to do my job," Comaneci announced when she arrived in Montreal with her teammates. She wound up putting in overtime.

The world was fascinated by Comaneci, but she was so young it learned little about her. She carried her Eskimo doll to news conferences, and confessed that her greatest wish was just to go home to Bucharest.

Four years later, Comaneci won two more gold medals—on the beam and the floor exercises—and finished second in the all-around. Romanian gymnastics was the best in the world, but there was tragedy behind the gold medals, and it turned out that Comaneci was one of the victims.

The life of the perfect 10 was far from perfect. Writers who visited her in Bucharest later described her with symptoms of anorexia and bulimia, purging herself in the midst of dinners to keep her weight down. She was a frequent companion—forced, she would write years later—of the son of Nicolae Ceausescu, the Romanian tyrant. And when Ceausescu's dictatorship ended in the revolution of 1989, Comaneci crawled on her hands and knees through the mud, first to Hungary and then Austria, and fled to the United States.

She sold her life story and worked as a model, posing for an underwear ad on a huge billboard in Times Square. She eventually settled down—in the United States, with another gold-medal gymnast, Bart Connor.

A perfect ending.

CHAPTER XVIII

Once and Future Champions?

Pick an Olympics, any Olympics, and you can pretty well match it with an individual who was the brightest star of an intense constellation.

In 1912, it was Jim Thorpe. In 1936, it was Jesse Owens. In 1968, in was Bob Beamon. In 1972, it was Mark Spitz. In 1976, it was Nadia Comaneci.

Who will be the star of 1996?

The Olympics always seem to produce surprises. But here are five athletes—two old-timers and three new faces—who have a chance to make Atlanta "their" Games.

KING CARL

"Where has the time gone?"

The question was posed rhetorically by Carl Lewis. But he knew as well as anyone where the last 15 years have been blown.

Into history. Into the record books.

By the time the flame is extinguished in Atlanta, Lewis will have been a member of his fifth U.S. Olympic team. He will have tried to add to a career that includes eight Olympic gold medals, eight world championships, 10 world records and 17 national titles.

For a decade and a half, Lewis has been the measure of world track-and-field greatness. He is, perhaps, the best athlete in history.

Longevity is one measure of that greatness. Lewis has been on the world stage since he and his sister, Carol, were high-school sensations in the Philadelphia suburb of Willingboro, New Jersey, in the late 1970s. He won his first major national title in 1980, taking the NCAA indoor long jump championship in Detroit with a leap of 26 feet, 4 ⅝ inches. He has run and jumped through the Ben Johnson era, the Leroy Burrell era, the Linford Christie era, the Calvin Smith era, the Dennis Mitchell era, the Mike Powell era, the Robert Emmiyan era, the Larry Myricks era, the Joe DeLoach era. They all have become the "King Carl" era.

Versatility is another gauge. Lewis has been a world or national champion at 60, 100 and 200 meters, in the long jump and running relays. He has been ranked first in the world in all of his events at least twice. *Track and Field News*, the most prestigious journal of the sport in the United States, has voted him the world's Track and Field Athlete of the Year three times, the U.S. Athlete of the Year seven times and the Athlete of the Decade for the 1980s.

Consistency is a third. Lewis has been at the top of the sport since 1981, when he was ranked first in the world in the 100 and the long jump. Between 1981 and 1992, there was only one year when he was not ranked No. 1 in at least one of his specialties. That was 1991, when he was second in the 100 and long jump.

Finally, there is superiority. That is Lewis. Few humans have broken the 10-second barrier in the 100 meters; Lewis has done it more than 25 times. He has dipped below the 20-second barrier in the 200 eight times. On 10 occasions, he has anchored a 4-by-100 meter relay team to a time of 38 seconds or better, including six world records, and his anchor legs in the World Championships in 1983 and the Olympics in 1992 were legendary, awe-inspiring bursts of speed.

But if there is one place where Lewis has left his mark more than any other, it is in the long jump, the event he has won the last three Olympics and where he has his best hope for a gold medal in Atlanta.

Between March 13, 1981, when he won the NCAA Indoors with a leap of 27-10, and the 1991 World Championships, no one beat Carl Lewis in the long jump. That's a streak of 65 meets, a record, and it took a world-record jump of 29-4 ½ by Powell to finally end the run. Lewis topped 29 feet, too, at 29-2 ¾.

It's more than just the records and the championships that have defined the Lewis era. Always, there has been someone there to duel with.

Lewis was picked for the 1980 Olympic team but was denied the chance to compete because of the U.S. boycott. By the time the '84 Games were held in Los Angeles, Lewis was a world champion competing against a legend—Jesse Owens. The hype was Lewis' attempt to be the first Olympic athlete other than Owens to win gold medals in the 100, the 200, the long jump and the relay. It was a circus, with Lewis at his flamboyant best. He matched Owens' feat, even though he did upset more than a few people by taking only two attempts to get the long-jump gold. After anchoring the 400-meter relay for his fourth title, Lewis literally wrapped himself in the American flag on the victory lap.

At the Games in 1988, the opponent was Ben Johnson. He had beaten Lewis at the World Championships the previous summer with a world-record 9.83 in the 100, and Lewis was bitter, especially because he thought Johnson was using illegal drugs to boost performance. Johnson zoomed away in the Olympic 100, glancing over his shoulder as he beat Lewis in 9.79, but Lewis wound up with the gold—and the world record—when Johnson finally tested positive for steroids. Another nemesis down the tubes.

Bob Beamon's long-standing world record of 29-2 ¼ in the long jump was Lewis' next goal. Mike Powell got there first. But Lewis got revenge at the 1992 Olympics, winning the gold medal after a sub-par season in which he failed to make the Olympic team in the sprints.

Ghosts, drug-users, legends. All have been challenges to Lewis. And sometimes, his biggest challenge has been himself. Enigmatic is too shallow a word for Lewis' personality. He is a forceful, powerful athlete who is deeply sensitive. His Houston home contains an extensive collection of fine porcelain, and from his earliest days on the international track scene Lewis has been buffeted by questions about his sexual preference. Always he has waved off the speculation, but at times has seemed to court it. In the winter of 1994, for instance, a series of ads in Europe for a tire company featured Lewis in a skin-tight track suit, his buttocks high in the air and his feet encased in red high heels.

Who is this guy? Fans and competitors really don't know. Lewis doesn't drop many hints. He lets his running and jumping do the talking.

"At this stage in my career, I don't have to prove anything," Lewis said. "I am still running fast and I am optimistic about what I am doing. For the last five or six years, I've been taking it one year at a time. I have no reason to rush it. I like my 30s better than my 20s."

TAKING IT ALL IN STRIDE

Been there, done that. Jackie Joyner-Kersee has been through it all, from the exhilaration of a gold-medal performance to the pain of a pulled muscle just when another championship was within reach.

And whether she's standing on the medal podium with the prize around her neck, or bent over double trying just to fill her lungs and take not one more stride but one more step, she remembers: There are people out there watching. People out there who care. People to whom I mean something more than just a paycheck.

"Where I come from, it was a struggle," the woman known simply as JJK said. Jackie Joyner grew up on truly mean streets, in East St. Louis, Illinois. Track and field helped her get out.

"The young people back there don't think there is a way out," she said. "I want them to know there is. I worked hard to get where I am, and if they want to achieve great things, they need to continue to believe in God, believe in themselves, and continue to work hard. Nothing is going to come too easy. If you appreciate your struggles, you then go on to higher achievements."

Joyner-Kersee's life has been one high achievement after another. She has done something for women's track and field that perhaps no one else—not even Babe Didriksen or Fanny Blankers-Koen—could do. She has raised the consciousness of the average fan to appreciate that she is an athlete first, not a woman, and that her records and versatility mean as much as anything a man ever accomplished. They are something special.

"Her performances are like a great opera or concert," said Bob Kersee, her husband and coach. "I feel like I should be wearing a tux when I watch them."

Joyner-Kersee is the greatest female athlete in the world. She holds the world record in the heptathlon, the seven-event torture that is the women's equivalent of the decathlon, at 7,291 points at the 1988 Olympics. She won the 1992 gold medal, as well, at 7,044, and will be going for an unprecedented third in a row in Atlanta.

She's also pretty good in single events. In the long jump, she won the gold medal in 1988, a silver in '84 and the bronze in '92. She is a world-class sprinter and hurdler. One of her few recent disappointments came in the 1991 World Championships. She was leading the heptathlon when her right hamstring popped during the 200 meters. She fell—but she wasn't sure it was quite time to quit.

"I was thinking I could make it," Joyner-Kersee said.

Even though she will be 34 by the time the Atlanta Games begin, she keeps going and knowing that there are more goals to achieve, more records to conquer.

"She's getting better as she gets older," said Gail Devers, a teammate when both were UCLA students and the '92 Olympic champion in the 100 meters. "Age has nothing to do with it. It's mind over matter and it's wisdom, which comes with experience."

Such experience is what separates the 1996 version of JJK from the one who started her Olympic career in Los Angeles in 1984, where she finished second in the heptathlon by just five points to Glynnis Nunn of Australia.

"In 1984, I had the athletic skills to win a gold, but I didn't have the knowledge to pull it off," she said.

And so Atlanta offers a chance to redeem herself.

"I think I would retire," she said, "but the ultimate goal is to finish my Olympic career on American soil, to win a gold medal on U.S. soil."

AT HOME WITH MUFFIN AND SNOWBALL

As a veteran teen-ager, Jennie Thompson gives her sport the ultimate accolade.

"I think gymnastics," she says, "is better than going to the mall."

Thompson won't celebrate her 15th birthday until the Atlanta Olympics are 10 days old. But she is a good bet to carry on the medal-winning tradition started by Mary Lou Retton in 1984 and maintained by such other U.S. gymnastics stars as Shannon Miller and Dominique Dawes.

Thompson, all 4-foot-1 and 58 pounds of her, is the latest Olympic hopeful for Bela Karolyi, the coach who trained Nadia Comaneci in their native Romania and then helped turn Retton into a gold-medal star after defecting to the United States.

She worked at Karolyi's Gym in Houston, where Thompson was among a group of eighth-graders intent on perfecting their twists, turns and tumbles in a four-year program aimed directly at Atlanta. Thompson was at the head of her class. She became the youngest U.S. junior national event champion, on the floor exercise, as a 12-year-old in 1992 and the following year became the youngest all-around junior champ, at 13.

She began competing internationally in 1991, when she was 10, and in '94 went to St. Petersburg, Russia, for the Goodwill Games. There was a special prize for her there—a vase from the city, an award for being the youngest competitor at the games.

"Pretty neat," in Jennie's words.

That's pretty much Thompson's story all around, according to her coaches.

"She has a tremendous concentration ability for her age," said Achim Fassbender, one of the Karolyi center's coaches. "When we went to the (junior) Pan American Games (in Brazil in 1992, where Thompson won the all-around gold medal), it was fantastic to see how she could totally focus and pull the performances out of that concentration."

Thompson was born on July 29, 1981, in Wichita Falls, Texas, and began gymnastics in 1986. Her favorite apparatus is the uneven bars.

"My brother Matthew started taking gymnastics first," she said. "I would go and watch him. I thought it was fun."

At age 8, she joined Karolyi's gym in Houston. Since then, it's been training five days a week—7-8:15 a.m. and 3-8 p.m. Mondays, Wednesdays and Fridays, with just the afternoon sessions Tuesdays and Thursdays.

"Nobody wakes them up," said Dennis Thompson, Jennie's father. "By the time they wake me up, they're ready to go."

School is at a private Christian academy that accommodates their gymnastics schedule.

"I go at 8:30, so I miss a couple of minutes," Jennie said. "And I miss my last period of the day."

Workouts consist of flexing, vaults, tumbling, chin-ups, inverted hangs and leg-lifts. There's also dancing and work on individual apparatus stations.

At home, schoolwork and snacks take up most of the time between practices. There's also a few minutes to spend with Muffin and Snowball, her cats. Saturdays and Sundays are set aside for time with family and friends.

"Everyone at school says, 'Well, you don't have time to go out or anything,'" Thompson said. "But we can always do that on weekends."

And remember—you hardly ever find a good sale on gold medals at the mall.

A BREATH OF FRESH AIR

For Tom Dolan, swimming is easy. Breathing is hard.

Dolan is a world champion, winning the title in the 400-meter individual medley in Rome in 1994 in a world-record time of 4 minutes, 13.52 seconds.

He's a world-class freestyler at distances from 400-1,500 meters, and the winner of four titles at the 1994 Spring Nationals, the first American to do that since Mark Spitz in 1972. That earned him '94 Swimmer of the Year honors.

And he's one of the favorites to help American men continue their domination of the Olympic swimming events.

What makes all this more remarkable is that there are times when Dolan can hardly catch a breath. At 13, Dolan, from Arlington, Virginia, was diagnosed with exercise-induced asthma.

"As a little kid, I had a lot of allergies," he said.

Swimming short distances was OK. But once Dolan stepped up to longer races, like the 800 freestyle, things changed. Breathing and swimming became more complicated. And the summer of '94 became his worst yet.

"I'd go to meets and have trouble. I wouldn't even be thinking about swimming," he said. "I was just trying to make it through. It's hard to explain, but it's just like having NO air."

The problem got so bad that Dolan went to see a pulmonary specialist. "They stuck a tiny little black tube with a camera on it down the back of my throat," he said. "What they saw was that the size of my esophagus was too small."

Doctors estimate that Dolan can inhale only 20 percent of the oxygen a normal human can gulp. Treating asthma is tough enough for the average person. For an athlete, it's downright near impossible. Remember Rick Demont? He lost an Olympic gold medal in 1972 for using a prescription asthma medicine that contained a banned stimulant.

So Dolan must compete while using watered-down asthma sprays and hope he can control his illness while also controlling the competition.

Dolan has been swimming since he was 5 and began swimming year-round at age 7. He came up through U.S. Swimming Federation camps and age-group teams and joined the Curl-Burke Swim Club in his hometown. He also enrolled at the University of Michigan, where strength work complemented the pool practice he was getting at club level.

213

If there was a body built for swimming, it would be Dolan's. He is 6-foot-6, weighs 180 pounds and carries between 2-3 percent body fat. And this from a guy who says he can eat anything.

Take this typical menu from his days at Michigan:

"I'd have three or four plates of pasta, a loaf of bread and two bowls of ice cream at dinner," Dolan said. "Then, a few hours later, after I've done my homework, I'd go over to the student union and get a foot-long sub."

Subs for snacks. No wonder he's so good in the water.

GOING THE DISTANCE

In 1964, Bob Schulz and Billy Mills of the United States swept the two longest races on the Olympic track, the 5,000 and 10,000 meters. Since then, no American man has taken home so much as a bronze medal from an Olympic distance race.

That may be about to change in Atlanta. Meet Bob Kennedy, who has charged out of Indiana to take a place among the best distance runners in the world.

Kennedy had been on the heels of the distance terrors from Ethiopia, Kenya and Morocco for some time before the summer of 1994. Then, in two European races in the space of two weeks, he twice lowered the mark for the fastest time ever in the 5,000 by a native-born American runner, first to 13 minutes, 5.93 seconds, then to 13:02.93, the ninth-fastest time in history.

Both races were won by Khalid Skah, the defending Olympic 10,000-meter champion from Morocco. But Kennedy saw more than just a pair of second-place finishes. "This makes me a legitimate Olympic medal contender," he said. "Anyone under 13:10 is a legitimate threat."

For a distance runner, an Olympic win means big money. And for an American to win in an Olympics in the United States would make it even bigger, in Kennedy's estimation.

"If I were to win an Olympic gold medal in Atlanta, that's a million dollars," he said.

Kennedy comes from a running family. His father, Bob Sr., was a three-mile champion at Indiana. "He never pushed me into running," the younger Kennedy said, "but he said, 'Whatever you do, try to be the best.'"

His quest for that goal may have been helped by an injury in March 1994. He suffered a stress fracture and was told to take a month off. When he came back, he felt rejuvenated and started clipping big chunks off his personal bests.

"The Kenyans take two months off at the end of every season," Kennedy said. "No American does that." He learned another lesson in European training sessions with the African runners, the long-distance trend-setters. "You realize they're not super-human," he said.

After his first Olympic experience, Kennedy felt almost sub-human. He finished 12th in the 5,000 at Barcelona, a disappointing showing for the two-time NCAA cross-country champion. He decided that the 60 miles a week of training runs he was putting in just were not enough.

Now, he's up to 90-95 miles a week in the off-season, with a "long" run of 12 miles at a pace of 6-6 ½ minutes per mile. "Maybe at some point I'll need to do more to improve," he said, "but not right now."

Having been through the Olympics once, Kennedy also knows that success at the Games depends on more than just how you prepare physically.

"Going into the Olympics, people say there's a lot of pressure. You tend to say, 'That won't bother me.' But you can't help but be overwhelmed," he said. "It won't happen again. ... I've got a better idea now what it takes to be on top. Basically, you have to be ready to run as hard as you can from the gun."

Before Kennedy heads off to Atlanta, he has one last word: Don't talk to him about the joy of a "runner's high" or the lilting feeling of hitting "the Wall."

"Running is not any fun," he said. "It's probably the only physical activity that hurts the whole time you're doing it. I don't see myself doing it when I'm 40. I only do it now because it makes me better. And I love the competition. I love winning."

AND THEN THERE'S .....

A number of other athletes from around the world are likely to make an impact at the Games. Here are some of them:

Track:

Nourredine Morceli, Algeria. World record holder at three classic distances, the mile, the 1,500 and the 3,000, he is the best distance runner in the world and the latest African athlete to dominate the long races.

Qu Yanxia and Wang Junxia, China. Members of "Mao's Army," the group of women runners who lowered world records to unheard-of lows in the summer of 1993. Qu holds the world record in the 1,500, while Wang is the world's fastest at 10,000. They are far and away the best in the world in their events.

Swimming:

Kieran Perkins, Australia. The 1992 gold medalist in the men's 1,500 freestyle, he holds world records in the 400, 800 and 1,500 freestyle. The most dominant swimmer in the world today.

Jingyi Li, China. The winner of five gold medals in the last World Championship in 1994, she holds the world record in the women's 50-meter and 100-meter freestyle.

Gymnastics:

Ivan Ivankov, Belarus. The world men's all-around champion in 1994, his strengths are on the high bar, the vault and the uneven bars. Another champion produced by the old Soviet sports machine.

Lavinia Milosovici, Romania. A powerful gymnast with strengths in the floor exercise and vault. Milosovici was the silver medalist in women's all-around at the 1994 world championships behind American Shannon Miller.

Diving:

Dimitri Sautin, Russia. The best all-around diver in the world, Sautin won the platform gold medal at the 1994 world championships and the silver in the 3-meter springboard. He was a bronze medalist in the springboard at the 1992 Olympics.

Fu Mingxia and Tang Shuping, China. These two teen-agers are the Chinese equivalent of Sautin. Fu is the defending Olympic gold medalist in the platform, while Tang won the springboard world championship in 1994.

Basketball:

Tony Kukoc, Croatia. After leading his country to the silver medal behind the U.S. "Dream Team" in 1992, Kukoc signed with the professional Chicago Bulls for one of the biggest contracts in NBA history. He is a strong, quick forward with ball-handling abilities that once won him the nickname, "the Magic Johnson of Europe."

Hortencia Marcari, Brazil. The Reggie Miller of women's hoops, Hortencia is a veteran guard who loves to shoot. She scored 32 points against the United States in the women's world championships in 1994.

CHAPTER XIX

Top Ten Teams

Almost 200 nations will send athletes to Atlanta. Less than 10 percent of that number will win more than a handful of medals.

Changes in world sports—the breakup of the East bloc, the addition of professionals, the emergence of countries such as South Korea and China—make predictions iffy.

Nevertheless, here's a fearless attempt to handicap what should be the Top Ten in Atlanta:

1. **United States**—Hosting an Olympics does something to a nation's athletes. It makes every event a home game, for one thing, and the team benefits from increased funding and less time away from family and friends. Every time the United States has hosted an Olympics, Winter or Summer, it has turned in its best showing, and Atlanta should be no exception. The team is loaded.

   Track and field is strong from the sprints on up, with new challengers in the distance and field events. Women's swimming may be second in the world to the Chinese, but the U.S. men still dominate. The men's basketball team—no, it won't be called Dream Team III—won't be as strong as the 1992 edition, but it's still a lock for the gold. The women's hoop team should challenge too. Cycling, canoeing, archery and shooting are among the smaller sports in which the U.S. team is strong. And look for at least two gold medals in tennis, probably from Pete Sampras in men's singles and the Jensen brothers in men's doubles. The U.S. Olympic Committee is putting a major effort into this team, including an Operation Gold package that offers $15,000 for a gold medal, and this should pay off in a gold rush. Look for 1996 to be the first time since 1984—and the first Olympics with a full, non-boycott field since 1968—that the USA leads the medals table.

2. **Russia**—The remnants of the old sports machine of the Soviet Union still turn out some of the world's best athletes. Russians are strong in track, rowing, cycling, shooting, weightlifting and wrestling. Their men's swimming team, led by sprinter Alexandr Popov, will challenge the U.S. supremacy. And their gymnasts remain the best in the world.

3. **China**—Maybe it's drugs. Maybe it's worm soup. Maybe it's just a fact that in a nation of more than a billion people, you're going to find great athletes. Whatever the reason, the Chinese team for '96 will be the most imposing the country has sent to the Olympics so far. Women's sports are especially strong, with swimming, diving and distance running capable of producing up to 15 gold medals.

4. **Germany**—The "super team" many expected when East and West Germany reunited has not materialized and may never exist. Germany, however, is strong in equestrianism, field hockey, team handball, swimming, fencing, canoeing and rowing. Track should produce a few golds and men's basketball could provide a surprise bronze.

5. **Cuba**—Take the baseball team. Add the boxers. Right there, Cuba has as many as 10 gold medals. The Cubans also are contenders in track, wrestling and volleyball.

6. **Australia**—Always a well-rounded team with its share of medals, the Australian squad will be its biggest ever as it begins the buildup for the 2000 Games in Sydney. Look for strength in swimming, track, cycling and kayaking.

7. **South Korea**—This country's athletes benefitted immensely from hosting the 1988 Summer Games, finding world-class training and competition facilities suddenly available and a slew of traditional sports added to the Olympic program. Tae kwan do, the national martial art, is now a medal sport. That should send lots of gold back to Seoul.

8. **Hungary**—The emerging power of the old East bloc, Hungary is producing top-flight athletes across the board. Swimming, fencing and women's gymnastics are strong points.

9. **Spain**—As hosts in '92, the Spanish were the surprise of Barcelona, finishing 10th with a record 13 gold medals. They may not produce as many champions in Atlanta, but overall their team is deep, particularly in swimming and yachting.

10. **Britain**—Put two asterisks on this. One is for age—some of the Brits' biggest stars in '92, such as hurdler Sally Gunnell and sprinter Linford Christie, are getting old. The second is for drugs—Britain's sports programs, especially track and field, have been mauled by positive drug tests in recent years. If they can avoid those hurdles, they will show surprisingly well.

CHAPTER XX

Olympics: The Second 100 Years

On the evening of Sunday, August 4, 1996, this big birthday party will end.

The men's marathon winner will be crowned, the athletes will parade into the Olympic stadium for one last time. IOC President Juan Antonio Samaranch almost surely will proclaim the Atlanta Games "the best ever."

The big white Olympic flag will be lowered and passed to officials from Sydney, Australia, where the Olympics will welcome the new millennium in 2000. The flame atop that tall pedestal beyond right-centerfield wall will be extinguished.

Atlanta will be just Atlanta again. But the Olympics will go on in other places, with other issues.

First comes Nagano, Japan, the site of the 1998 Winter Games. They will be expensive for athletes and fans, but it's virtually certain they will maintain the artistic and financial success that the Olympic community has created over the last dozen years.

Likewise, Sydney will bring its own magic to the Games, welcoming the world's youth Down Under for the first time in almost half a century.

From there, it might be back to the United States. Salt Lake City's bid was a favorite for the 2002 Winter Games. South Africa and Puerto Rico were among countries willing to bid for the Summer Olympics in 2004. And from there ...

The movement that was on its deathbed in the 1970s is thriving. It also has problems, including how big it should be and who should lead it. Samaranch is getting old and has said he would not run for another term after Atlanta, but no clearcut successor has emerged. It could be Dick Pound of Canada, or Un Young Kim of South Korea, or one of a pair of fast-rising Europeans, Thomas Bach or Jacques Rogge.

No matter who, the next IOC chief will face problems of money, doping and internal strife. He or she will have to contend with the growing problem of violence in sports. And with the amateur world gone and U.S. college athletes clamoring for a part of the billion-dollar contracts they help their universities attract from TV and sponsors, how long will it be before Olympic athletes demand a piece of the pie, too?

But rest assured the Olympics will go on. The flame will burn, and for two weeks every two years, the world will seem just a little smaller.

And a little better.

APPENDIX

SUMMER OLYMPIC RECORDS

Archery, Shooting, Swimming, Track and Field, Weightlifting

(NOTE: These are the only summer sports for which Olympic performance records are maintained.)

ARCHERY

Women

	Points	Name, Country	Date Record Set
Individual	2,568	Hyang-Soon Seo, Korea	8/11/84
	344*	Soo-Nyung Kim, Korea	9/30/88
Team Competition	982	Soo-Nyung Kim/Hee-Kyung Wang/ Young-Sook Yun, Korea	

Men

	Points	Name, Country	Date Record Set
Individual	2,616	Darrell Pace, USA	8/11/84
	338*	Jay Barrs, USA	9/30/88
Team Competition	986	In-Soo Chun/Han-Sup Lee/ Sung-Soo Park, Korea	

* New under Grand FITA

SHOOTING
Women

Event	Points	Name Country,	Date Record Set
Air Rifle	396/400	Vesela Letcheva, Bulgaria	7/26/92
		Kab-Soon Yeo, Korea	7/26/92
w/finals	498.2 (396+102.2)	Kab-Soon Yeo, Korea	7/26/92
Standard Rifle	587/600	Launi Meili, USA	7/30/92
w/finals	684.3 (587+97.3)	Launi Meili, USA	7/30/92
Sport Pistol	597/600	Marina Logvinenko, Unified Team	7/27/92
w/finals	684 (587+97)	Marina Logvinenko, Unified Team	7/27/92
Air Pistol	389/400	Jasna Sekaric, IOP	8/1/92
w/finals	486.4 (387+99.4)	Marina Logvinenko, Unified Team	8/1/92
	486.4 (389+97.4)	Jasna Sekaric, IOP	8/1/92

Men

Event	Points	Name Country,	Date Record Set
Air Rifle	593/600	Jury Fedkin, Unified Team	7/27/92
w/finals	695.3 (593+102.3)	Jury Fedkin, Unified Team	7/27/92
Free Pistol	581	Aleksandr Melentev, Russia	7/20/80
w/finals	660 (566+94)	Sorin Babii, Romania, 9/18/88	
Smallbore Rifle			
Prone	598/600	Hubert Bichler, Germany	7/29/92
w/finals	702.5 (597+105.5)	Eun-Chul Lee, Korea	7/29/92
Smallbore Rifle 3			
Positions	1,172/1,200	Juha Uirvi, Finland	7/31/92
w/finals	1,267.4 (1,169+98.4)	Gracha Petikian, EUN	7/31/92
Rapid Fire Pistol	594/600	Ralph Schumann, Germany	7/30/92
w/finals	885 (594+195+96)	Ralph Schumann, Germany	7/30/92

Event	Time	Name, Country	Date Record Set
Running Game			
Target	580/600	Michael Jakosits, Germany	8/1/92
w/finals	673 (580 + 93)	Michael Jakosits, Germany	8/1/92
Air Pistol	586/600	Sorin Babii, Romania	7/28/92
w/finals	684.8 (585+99.8)	Yifu Wang, China	7/28/92
Mixed			
Trap Shooting	196/200	Pavel Kubec, Czechoslovakia	8/2/92
w/finals	219 (195 + 24)	Petr Hrdlicka, Czechoslovakia	8/2/92
Skeet Shooting	200/200	Shan Zhang, China	7/28/92
w/finals	223 (200 + 23)	Shan Zhang, China	7/28/92

SWIMMING
Women

Event	Time	Name, Country	Date Record Set
50 m Freestyle	24.79	Yang Wenji, China	7/31/92
100 m Freestyle	54.64	Zhuang Yong, China	7/26/92
200 m Freestyle	1:57.65	Heike Friedrich, East Germany	9/21/88
400 m Freestyle	4:03.85	Janet Evans, USA	9/22/88
800 m Freestyle	8:20.20	Janet Evans, USA	9/24/88
100 m Backstroke	1:00.68	Krisztina Egerszegi, Hungary	7/28/92
200 m Backstroke	2:07.06	Krisztina Egerszegi, Hungary	7/31/92
100 m Breaststroke	1:07.95	Tania Dangalakova, Bulgaria	9/23/88
200 m Breaststroke	2:26.65	Kyoko Iwasaki, Japan	7/27/92
100 m Butterfly	58.62	Hong Qian, China	7/29/92
200 m Butterfly	2:06:90	Mary T. Meagher, USA	8/2/84
200 m Ind. Medley	2:11.65	Lin Li, China	7/30/92
400 m Ind. Medley	4:36.29	Petra Schneider, East Germany	7/26/80
4 x 100 m Freestyle Relay	3:39.46	Nicole Haislett, Dara Torres, Angel Martino, Jenny Thompson, USA	7/28/92
4 x 100 m Medley Relay	4:02.54	Lea Loveless, Anita Nall, Crissy Ahmann-Leighton, Jenny Thompson, USA	7/30/92

Men

Event	Time	Name, Country	Date Record Set
50 m Freestyle	21.91	Alexander Popov, Unified Team	7/30/92
100 m Freestyle	48.63	Matthew Biondi, USA	9/22/88
200 m Freestyle	1:46.70	Evgueni Sadovyi, Unified Team	7/26/92
400 m Freestyle	3:45.00	Evgueni Sadovyi, Unified Team	7/29/92
1,500 m Freestyle	14:43.48	Kieren Perkins, AUS	7/31/92
100 m Backstroke	53.98	Mark Tewksbury, Canada	7/30/92
200 m Backstroke	1:58.47	Martin Lopez-Zubero, Spain	7/28/92
100 m Breaststroke	1:01.50	Nelson Diebel, USA	7/26/92
200 m Breaststroke	2:10.16	Mike Barrowman, USA	7/29/92
100 m Butterfly	53.00	Anthony Nesty, Suriname	9/21/88
200 m Butterfly	1:56.26	Melvin Stewart, USA	7/30/92
200 m Ind. Medley	2:00.17	Tamas Darnyi, Hungary	9/25/88
400 m Ind. Medley	4:14.23	Tamas Darnyi, Hungary	7/27/92
4 x 100 m Freestyle Relay	3:16.53	Christopher Jacobs, Troy Dalbey, Thomas Jager, Matthew Biondi, USA	9/23/88
4 x 200 m Freestyle Relay	7:11.95	Dmitri Lopikov, Vladimir Pychnenko, Veniamin Taianovitch, Evgueni Sadovyi, Unified Team	7/27/92
4 x 100 m			

Event	Time	Name, Country	Date Record Set
Medley Relay	3:36.93	David Berkoff, Richard Schroeder, Matthew Biondi, Christopher Jacobs, USA	9/25/88
		Jeff Rouse, Nelson Diebel, Pablo Morales, Jon Olsen, USA,	7/31/92

TRACK AND FIELD
Women

Event	Time	Name, Country	Date Record Set
100 meters	10.54	Florence Griffith Joyner, USA	9/25/88
200 meters	21.34	Florence Griffith Joyner, USA	9/29/88
400 meters	48.65	Olga Bryzguina, Russia	9/26/88
800 meters	1:53.43	Nadezhda Olizarenko, USSR	7/27/80
1,500 meters	3:53.96	Paula Ivan, Romania	10/01/88
3,000 meters	8:26.53	Tatiana Samolenko, Russia	9/25/88
10,000 meters	31:05.21	Olga Bondarenko, Russia	9/30/88
100 m Hurdles	12.38	Jordanka Donkova, Bulgaria	9/30/88
400 m Hurdles	53.17	Debra Flintoff-King, Australia	9/28/88
4 x 100 meters	41.60	Romy Muller, Barbel Wockel, Ingrid Auerswald, Marlies Gohr, East Germany	8/1/80
4 x 400 meters	3:15.18	Tatiana Ledovskaia, Olga Nazarova, Maria Piniguina, Olga Bryzguina, Russia	10/01/88
10 km Walk	44:32	Yueling Chen, China	8/3/92
High Jump	2.03 m (6'8")	Louise Ritter, USA	9/30/88
Long Jump	7.40 m (24' 3-1/2")	Jackie Joyner-Kersee, USA	9/29/88
Shot Put	22.41 m (73' 6-1/4")	Ilona Slupianek, East Germany	7/24/80
Discus	72.30 m (237' 2")	Martina Hellmann, East Germany	9/29/88
Javelin	74.68 m (245' 0")	Petra Felke, East Germany	9/26/88
Heptathlon	7,291 pts	Jackie Joyner-Kersee, USA	9/23-24/88
Marathon	2:24:52	Joan Benoit, USA	8/5/84

Men

Event	Time	Name, Country	Date Record Set
100 meters	9.92	Carl Lewis, USA	9/24/88
200 meters	19.73	Mike Marsh, USA	8/5/92
400 meters	43.50	Quincy Watts, USA	8/5/92
800 meters	1:43.00	Joaquim Cruz, Brazil	8/6/84
1,500 meters	3:32.53	Sebastian Coe, Great Britain	8/11/84
5,000 meters	13:05.59	Said Aouita, Morocco	8/11/84
10,000 meters	27:21.46	Mly. Brahim Boutaib, Morocco	9/26/88
110 m Hurdles	12.98	Roger Kingdom, USA	9/26/88
400 m Hurdles	46.78	Kevin Young, USA	8/6/92
3,000m Steeplechase	8:05.51	Julius Karivki, Kenya	9/30/88
20 km Walk	1:19:57.0	Jozef Pribilinec, Czechoslovakia	9/23/88
50 km Walk	3:38:29	Viacheslav Ivanenko, Russia	9/30/88
Marathon	2:09:21.0	Carlos Lopes, Portugal	8/12/84
4 x 100 meters	37.40	Mike Marsh, Leroy Burrell, Dennis Mitchell, Carl Lewis, USA	8/8/92
4 x 400 meters	2:55.74	Andrew Valmon, Quincy Watts, MichaelJohnson, Steve Lewis, USA	8/8/92
High Jump	2.38m (7' 9-3/4")	Guennadi Avdeenko, Russia	9/25/88
Long Jump	8.90m (29' 2-1/2")	Bob Beamon, USA	10/18/68
Triple Jump	17.63m (59' 7-1/2")	Micheal Conley, USA	8/3/92
Pole Vault	5.90 m (19' 4-1/4")	Sergey Bubka, Russia	9/28/88
Shot Put	22.47m (73' 8-3/4")	Ulf Timmermann, East Germany	9/23/88
Discus	68.82m (225' 9")	Jurgen Schult, EAst Germany	10/01/88
Javelin	94.58 m (old imp.)-(310' 4")	Miklos Nemeth, Hungary	7/25/76
	(new imp.)-89.66 m	Jan Zelezny, Czechoslovakia	8/8/92
Hammer Throw	84.80 m (278' 2")	Serguei Litvinov, Russia	9/26/88
Decathlon	8,847 pts	Daley Thompson, Great Brtain	8/8-9/84

WEIGHTLIFTING

Weight Class	Lift	Name, Country	Date Record Set
52 KG			
Snatch	120.0 KG	Svedalin Marinov, Bulgaria	9/18/88
Clean & Jerk	150.0 KG	Svedalin Marinov, Buglaria	9/18/88
		Ivan Ivanov, Bulgaria	7/26/92
Total	270.0 KG (595.0 lbs)	Svedalin Marinov, Bulgaria	9/18/88
56 KG			
Snatch	132.5 KG	Byung-Kwan Chun, Korea	7/27/92
Clean & Jerk	165.0 KG	Oxen Mirzoian, Russia	9/19/88
Total	292.5 KG (644 3/4 lbs)	Oxen Mirzoian, Russia	9/19/88
60 KG			
Snatch	142.5 KG	Naim Suleymanoglu, Turkey	7/28/92
Clean & Jerk	190.0 KG	Naim Suleymanoglu, Turkey	9/20/88
Total	342.5 KG (755.0 lbs)	Naim Suleymanoglu, Turkey	9/20/88
67.5 KG			
Snatch	155.0 KG	Israel Militossian, Unified Team	7/29/92
Clean & Jerk	195.0 KG	Yanko Roussev, Bulgaria	7/23/80
Total	342.5 KG (755.0 lbs)	Yanko Rusev, Bulgaria	7/23/80
75 KG			
Snatch	167.5 KG	Borislav Guidikov, Bulgaria	9/22/88
Clean & Jerk	207.5 KG	Borislav Guidikov, Bulgaria	9/22/88
Total	375.0 KG (826.5 lbs)	Borislav Guidikov, Bulgaria	9/22/80
82.5 KG			
Snatch	177.5 KG	Yurik Vardanyan, Russia	7/26/80
Clean & Jerk	222.5 KG	Yurik Vardanyan, Russia	7/26/80
Total	400.0 KG (881 3/4 lbs)	Yurik Vardanyan, Russia	7/26/80
90 KG			
Snatch	190.0 KG	Serguei Syrtsov, Unified Team	8/1/92
Clean & Jerk	225.0 KG	Anatoli Khrapatyi, Russia	9/25/88
Total	412.5 KG (909 1/4 lbs)	Anatoli Khrapatyi, Russia	9/25/88
		Kakhi Kakhiachvili, Unified Team	8/1/92
100 KG			
Snatch	190.0 KG	Pavel Kouznetsov, Russia	9/26/88
		Victor Tregoubov, Unified Team	8/2/92
Clean & Jerk	235.0 KG	Pavel Kouznetsov, Russia	9/26/88
Total	425.0 KG (936 3/4 lbs)	Pavel Kouznetsov, Russia	9/26/88
110 KG			
Snatch	210.0 KG	Yuri Zakharevitch, Russia	9/27/88
Clean & Jerk	245.0 KG	Yuri Zakharevitch, Russia	9/27/88
Total	455.0 KG (1003.0 lbs)	Yuri Zakharevitch, Russia	9/27/88
+110 KG			
Snatch	212.0 KG	Alexandre Kourlovitch, Russia	9/29/88
Clean & Jerk	255.0 KG	Vasili Alexeev, Russia	7/27/76
Total	462.5 KG	Alexandre Kourlovitch, Russia	9/29/88